D0154462

THE STRANGER
Humanity and the Absurd

TWAYNE'S MASTERWORK STUDIES
ROBERT LECKER, GENERAL EDITOR

THE STRANGER
Humanity and the Absurd

English Showalter, Jr.

TWAYNE PUBLISHERS
A Division of G. K. Hall & Co.

The Stranger: Humanity and the Absurd
English Showalter, Jr.

Twayne's Masterworks Studies No. 24

Copyright 1989 by G. K. Hall & Co.
All rights reserved.
Published by Twayne Publishers
A Division of G. K. Hall & Co.
70 Lincoln Street
Boston, MA 02111

Book production and design by Gabrielle B. McDonald
Copyediting supervised by Barbara Sutton
Typeset in 10/14 Sabon
by Compset, Inc., Beverly, Massachusetts

Printed on permanent/durable acid-free paper
and bound in the United States of America

Library of Congress Cataloging–in–Publication Data
Showalter, English.
    The stranger.

    (Twayne's masterwork studies, no. 24)
    Bibliography: p.
    Includes index.
    1. Camus, Albert, 1913–1960. Stranger. I. Title.
PQ2605.A3734E874   1989   848'.91409   88-24391
ISBN 0-8057-7972-8
ISBN 0-8057-8022-X (pbk.)

CONTENTS

A NOTE ON THE REFERENCES AND ACKNOWLEDGMENTS

Quotations from *The Stranger* are from the excellent translation by Matthew Ward, published in 1988 by Alfred A. Knopf, with page numbers cited parenthetically. Because of its consistently greater fidelity to Camus's original French text, Ward's translation is far preferable to the earlier one by Stuart Gilbert, first published in 1946 in England and issued in paperback in 1954 by Vintage Books, a division of Random House. More than three million copies of Gilbert's translation have been sold in America, however, and because so many readers will probably still be using that edition, page references are given to it as well, following the initials "SG." Other French works are cited whenever possible from a published translation. If no translation is listed in the bibliography, the translation is my own and the reference is to the French edition. To keep the text as readable as possible, reference notes have been avoided. Full bibliographic information is given in the bibliography.

The frontispiece photograph of Camus was taken in 1957, on the occasion of his winning the Nobel Prize for literature. It is reprinted with the permission of the Bettmann Archive.

As always, I have received help from so many people that it hardly

A Note on the References and Acknowledgments

seems possible to name everyone. I would like especially to thank Tony Rizzuto for inviting me to participate in a colloquium on Camus at the State University of New York in Stony Brook in May 1987, and I should also thank the exceptional group of Camus scholars who took part and allowed me to share their good company as well as their knowledge: James Arnold, Peter Cryle, Brian Fitch, Raymond Gay-Crosier, Vicki Mistacco, Edouard Morot-Sir, Jean Sarocchi, Carl Viggiani, and Evelyn Zepp are notable among those who made that a memorable experience for me. My students at Rutgers, Camden, have challenged and stimulated me in ways that were particularly useful for a study of this sort, and Walter K. Gordon, dean of the Faculty of Arts and Sciences and provost of the Camden campus, has given me invaluable support. Finally, I owe my greatest gratitude to my family, Elaine, Vinca, and Michael; Camus readers all, they have helped me in many ways, but more important, they make me feel that it is all worth the trouble.

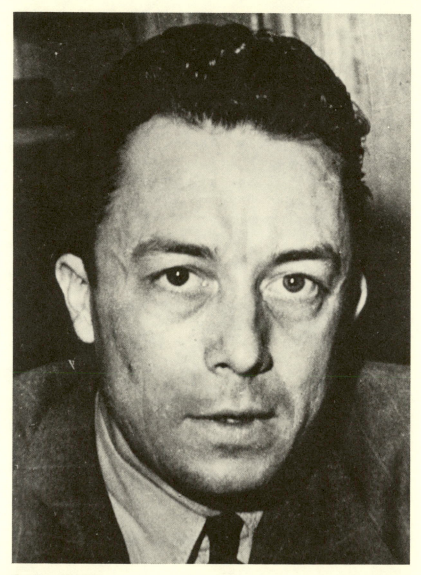

Albert Camus (1913–1960)
Photograph courtesy of the Bettman Archives.

CHRONOLOGY: ALBERT CAMUS'S LIFE AND WORKS

In addition to dates and events relating directly to Camus's life and career, this chronology mentions key moments in the principal historical events that concerned him: World War II, the cold war, the Algerian conflict. As a journalist, moralist, and thinker, an *écrivain engagé*, or "committed" writer, Camus experienced these traumatic events not only by living through them, but also and more importantly by writing about them, taking public positions on them, and trying to interpret them for his contemporaries as well as for readers in years to come.

1913   Albert Camus born 7 November in Mondovi, Algeria, at that time administratively a part of France. Second son of Lucien Auguste Camus, whose grandparents had emigrated to Algeria from Bordeaux shortly after the French conquest in 1830, and of Catherine Sintes, whose grandparents had emigrated from the Spanish island Minorca around the same time. Father employed by a wine producer; mother unable to read or write.

1914   Assassination of Archduke Ferdinand in Sarajevo, 28 June, precipitating World War I. Lucien Auguste Camus recalled for military service in the First Regiment of Zouaves, or North African troops. Family returns to Algiers, staying with maternal grandmother, Marie Catherine (Cardona) Sintes, in Belcourt, a working-class district.

| | Death of Camus's father, 11 October, from wounds suffered in the First Battle of the Marne. Mother suffers an attack, perhaps meningitis or perhaps shock, leaving her with partial deafness and a mild speech impairment. |

1914–1920 Albert, his older brother, Lucien (born 1910), his mother, his uncles, Étienne and Joseph Sintes, and his grandmother, live in a three-room (plus kitchen) apartment, without running water or electricity, sharing a toilet with three other apartments on the same floor. Mother works as cleaning woman. Boys raised by grandmother, stern disciplinarian, who whips them.

1918–1923 Camus attends the local public school, where a teacher, Louis Germain, takes a special interest in him, gives him extra instruction, and encourages him to compete for a scholarship at the *lycée* (high school) of Algiers.

1920 Uncle Joseph moves out; Étienne remains, and at an unknown date breaks up a romance between Camus's mother and an unidentified man. This incident, and many anecdotes and impressions of life in Belcourt, become the source material for much of Camus's fiction.

1923–1932 Scholarship student at the Algiers *lycée*. Strong interest in sports; plays goalie for soccer team. Attracts attention of another teacher, Jean Grenier, who exercises strong influence on his thought and remains a lifelong friend.

1930 First symptoms of tuberculosis.

1931 For health reasons Camus moves to home of aunt and uncle, Gustave and Antoinette (Sintes) Acault. Acault, a butcher but well-read, gives Camus books. Camus reads Gide, Malraux, Montherlant. Death of Grandmother Sintes.

1932–1933 Studies philosophy under Grenier, publishes articles in a local literary journal, *Sud*.

1933 Enters university in Algiers; joins in antifascist activities. Hitler comes to power in Germany.

1934 Marries Simone Hié, a fellow student, 16 June. The couple is supported by her mother, a doctor, and by income from his various jobs, including as a clerk in a shipping office and in the local drivers' license bureau. Joins Communist party. Is exempted from military service because of his lungs.

1935 Trip to Balearic Islands with Simone. Works on first book, a collection of essays and sketches called *L'Envers et l'endroit* (The wrong side and the right side).

1936 Founds the Théâtre du Travail; first play, an adaptation of

Malraux's antifascist novel, *Le Temps du mépris (Days of Wrath)*; the troupe's collectively written *Révolte dans les Asturies (Revolt in the Asturias)* banned. Completes work on his diploma with a thesis on philosophy, but health bars him from a teaching career. Trip to Europe, during which his marriage to Simone breaks up. On return, pursues work at the theatre and continues propaganda activities for the Communist party. Electoral success of the Popular Front, an alliance of leftist parties, including the Communist.

1937   Publication of *L'Envers et l'endroit*. Trip to Europe for health. Works as actor for Radio Algiers. Is expelled from Communist party because of disagreement with its decision to discontinue anticolonialist campaigning among Moslems, a disenfranchised and impoverished group constituting about 90 percent of the Algerian population. Works as a journalist for *Alger républicain*, a newly founded liberal newspaper. Continues theatrical activity in the Théâtre de l'Équipe, successor to the Théâtre du Travail. Reads intensely in modern philosophy, especially Nietzsche.

1938   Reviews Sartre's *La Nausée (Nausea)*; reads extensively; writes works that will become *L'Étranger (The Stranger)*, *Caligula*, and *Le Mythe de Sisyphe (The Myth of Sisyphus)*. Popular Front collapses, government turns to the right. Munich accord, appeasing Hitler, 30 September.

1939   Reports on poverty in Kabylie for *Alger républicain*. World War II begins with German invasion of Poland, 1 September. France declares war, 3 September. Camus attempts to enlist, is refused because of his health. *Alger républicain* closes.

1940   Goes to Paris to work for *Paris-Soir* in March. German invasion of France, 12 May; French surrender 17 June. Germans occupy only northern half of France; southern half administered by Vichy government, headed by Pétain, sympathetic to fascist policies. *Paris-Soir* moves south, but Camus dismissed in December because of staff cuts. Marriage in Lyons 3 December to Francine Faure, from Oran, Algeria; they had met in 1937 in Algiers.

1941   Returns to Oran, works as a teacher, publisher's reader; intensive work on his own writing.

1942   *The Stranger* published in July in Paris. Camus goes to south of France to recover from attack of tuberculosis. Wife returns to Oran, and before Camus can join her, Allies begin operations in North Africa, making travel impossible.

1943	Publishes *The Myth of Sisyphus*, an essay on the philosophy of the absurd. Works actively in a Resistance organization publishing the clandestine newspaper *Combat*. Moves to Paris, becomes a reader for the publisher Gallimard.
1944	Meets Sartre, other well-known writers and intellectuals. Liberation of Paris 24 August. Camus becomes editor of *Combat*, now a regular newspaper of the non-Communist left. *Le Malentendu (The Misunderstanding)*, a play, produced.
1945	Armistice in Europe 8 May. Camus engaged mostly in journalism in a difficult political climate, with France devastated by war and torn between factions. Birth of twin children. Production of *Caligula*, a play based on the Roman emperor, written before the war. Atom bomb dropped on Hiroshima 6 August. Surrender of Japan 2 September. France soon embroiled in a war with nationalists in French Indochina (Vietnam, Cambodia, and Laos).
1946	Trip to the United States; warm reception. October, verdicts in the Nuremberg trials of Nazi war criminals; execution of major Nazi leaders. Approval of a new French constitution, creating the Fourth Republic.
1947	Publishes *La Peste (The Plague)*, a symbolic novel about the bubonic plague, set in Oran; immediate success. Leaves *Combat*. Inauguration of the Marshall Plan for reconstructing Europe; hardening of opposition between Communist East and non-Communist West.
1948	Engages in political polemics. Production of *L'État de siège (State of Siege)*, an allegorical play about the plague, written in collaboration with actor-director Jean-Louis Barrault; poorly received. Berlin blockade, July.
1949	Trip to South America, with negative effects on Camus's health. Production of *Les Justes (The Just Assassins)*, a play about Russian anarchists of 1905. End of Berlin blockade, May. First atomic explosion in the Soviet Union, September.
1950	Publishes *Actuelles I*, collection of prose pieces, chiefly editorials and political journalism, from the period 1944–48. Beginning of the Korean War, as North Korean forces invade South Korea in June. American troops sent in response, with

	United Nations backing; Chinese troops cross the border in November.
1951	Publishes *L'Homme révolté (The Rebel)*, a philosophical essay on revolt, leading to a yearlong polemic and a break with Sartre and most of the Marxist left.
1953	Publishes *Actuelles II*, covering the period 1948–53. Armistice in Korea, July. Riots in East Berlin crushed by Russian troops.
1953–1956	Travels in Italy, Greece, and Algeria; writes briefly for the newsweekly *L'Express*; adapts various works for the stage.
1954	February to May, battle of Dien Bien Phu, ending French power in Southeast Asia. The Treaty of Paris, creating North and South Vietnam, signed in November. Nasser becomes premier of Egypt, April. Demands for independence from European domination growing stronger throughout North Africa: Libya independent since 1952, Tunisia autonomous in July 1954, riots in Morocco. November, Fellagha, or Moslem, leaders carry out their threat of armed revolt against France, beginning a war of terrorism and police reprisals that does not end until after Camus's death, with the independence of Algeria in 1962, under de Gaulle and the Fifth Republic.
1956	Publishes *La Chute (The Fall)*, an ironic confessional novel, thought by some to be his greatest work. Autumn, France, Great Britain, and Israel seize Suez, but withdraw. Revolt in Hungary, crushed by Russian troops.
1957	Publishes *L'Exil et le royaume (Exile and the Kingdom)*, a collection of stories. Continues to adapt works for the theatre and to direct. Receives the Nobel Prize for literature.
1958	Publishes *Actuelles III*, essays on Algeria dating from 1939 to 1958. Terrorism and police repression in Algeria are at a peak; Camus's appeal for moderation is generally ignored in the press. De Gaulle returns to power.
1959	In ill health, but works on a new novel, *Le Premier Homme* (The first man), which is never completed.
1960	Killed instantly in an automobile accident, 4 January.

1
HISTORICAL CONTEXT

The story Albert Camus tells in *The Stranger* seems to bear no relation to the external world of history and politics. Certainly there is no trace of the world war that was raging in Europe and North Africa at the time the novel, set in Algeria and published in Paris, first appeared. To be sure, like any substantial work of literature, it was written some time before it was published. According to the evidence of his notebooks, the first inspiration for *The Stranger* came to Camus in August 1937, the manuscript was completed in May 1940, and the book was published in July 1942. There can hardly have been five years in human history when there was greater upheaval.

Well before 1937, however, the signs of impending conflict were obvious, and Camus had certainly taken notice. Adolf Hitler had come to power in Germany in 1933, and within months Camus had joined an antifascist campaign. In 1934 he joined the Communist party, which presented itself at that time as the most effective opposition to fascism. Hitler annexed the Rhineland in March 1936. The Spanish Civil War began in July the same year, opposing the right-wing loyalists led by General Francisco Franco and backed by Hitler, to the republicans backed by the Soviet Union and left-wing sympathizers around the world, including many notable writers like Ernest Hemingway and André Malraux. During this period Camus worked first as an actor and theater director; he wrote and tried to stage *Revolt in the Asturias,* a play supporting the Spanish republicans and the anti-fascist movement. In early 1937 he became a journalist for a local newspaper, *Alger républicain,* and made politics a particular specialty. Throughout this period, he was preparing for an advanced university degree in philosophy and belonged to the milieu of Algerian intellectuals; in that capacity he joined in signing manifestoes on the current political situation.

In short, *The Stranger*'s insulation from the international social and political conflicts of the time cannot be explained either by its having been written earlier or by Camus's lack of interest. Camus chose to write in a somewhat abstract, even allegorical, mode; the setting is almost incidental. The characters could be of almost any modern nationality, the time could be almost any year in the twentieth century, the place could be almost any large city with a beach and a hot climate. This abstraction undoubtedly facilitated publication of the novel in a Paris occupied by the German army, and it has certainly contributed to the novel's widespread accessibility and appeal. It should not, however, obscure the fact Camus drew on his lived experience to create a narrative profoundly responsive to the public attitudes of the time.

There are in fact many autobiographical elements, although one must not overstress their importance. All novelists imagine fictive events by combining fragments of real ones, either experienced or heard about. Camus never did the central act of the novel, shoot a stranger in cold blood, and he was never charged, arrested, or imprisoned for such a crime. He also never did the second most important act, attend his mother's funeral, because Catherine Camus outlived her son Albert. *The Stranger* is not by any stretch of the term an autobiographical novel. Yet Camus modeled Meursault on himself in certain respects, giving the fictional hero his own love of the sun and the sea, his easy charm with women, and his macho attitudes. Like Meursault, Camus had worked as a clerk in a shipping office. Meursault had never known his father, nor had Camus, because his father, Lucien Auguste Camus, was killed in World War I when Albert was an infant. In *The Stranger* Meursault recalls a story his mother told him about his father's witnessing an execution; in another work, Camus tells the same story about his own parents. The silence that Meursault ascribes to his mother recalls Camus's description of his own mother, who was nearly deaf. Moreover, her family's names, Cardona and Sintes, have been retained in *The Stranger* in Meursault's fiancée Marie Cardona and his friend Raymond Sintès. The passage in chapter 2 relating a typical Sunday in Algiers and other details of Meursault's life before his crime seem to derive from notes that Camus took about his own neighborhood and his own recollections of growing up in Algiers. In other words, Camus used material he had seen and known firsthand to give an air of authenticity to *The Stranger*.

What he wanted to express in his novel, however, came much more from his philosophical and literary studies than from an urge to immortalize his own past. In May 1936 he defended his dissertation on "Neo-Platonism and Christian Thought," contrasting the two classical philosophers Plotinus and Saint Augustine, who were, perhaps not by coincidence, North Africans, and received a "Diploma of Advanced Studies." He had intended to pursue his graduate study still further and obtain an *agrégation,* which is roughly equivalent to an American Ph.D., but the French government required that future professors (all of whom, under the French law, are educated at government expense and then become employees of the state-run educational system) have certifiably good health. Camus had tuberculosis, which was incurable at the time; he applied twice for permission to study for the *agrégation* and was twice refused. Traces of this frustration are visible in Meursault's sketchy account of his past.

Even though he was forced to give up his projected career as a professor of philosophy, Camus, of course, retained strong ideas about what he had read and continued to develop them. In the late 1940s, largely because of his friendship with Jean-Paul Sartre, Camus was labeled an existentialist. He vehemently denied the accuracy of the label; in 1945 he wrote, in a text cited in Roger Quilliot's Pléiade edition of Camus's theater and fiction: "Sartre is an existentialist, and the only book of ideas I have published, *The Myth of Sisyphus,* was directed against those philosophers called existentialists" (xxxiv). Although one must respect Camus's authority on this matter, the appellation reflects in part the accurate perception that Camus shared with Sartre and the other philosophers called existentialists a number of common concerns and positions. In very basic terms, existentialist philosophers attach primary importance to the here-and-now. They are opposed to essentialists, who give precedence to some transcendant quality—whether it be a platonic form, an ideal concept only imperfectly realized in any actual entity; a soul, an eternal and immaterial being that survives the death of the physical body; or some other privileged higher essence that is separated from a base material existence.

The great French scientist and philosopher of the seventeenth century, Blaise Pascal, belonged to this existentialist tradition; so did the Danish philosopher of the early nineteenth century, Søren Kierkegaard, and the mid-nineteenth-century German philosopher Friedrich Nietzsche. Camus studied all of their works intensely, and he was deeply moved by writers in the existentialist tradition, notably Fëdor Dostoyevski and Malraux. Sartre's first novel, *Nausea,* appeared in 1938 and Camus reviewed it for *Alger républicain.*

In *The Myth of Sisyphus* Camus does not bother to refute or criticize thinkers of the essentialist tradition; they are too far from his own sense of what is self-evident. But he objects to the conclusions that many of the existentialists reach; Pascal, Kierkegaard, and Dostoyevski, for example, analyze the human condition and find such misery that philosophical choice is reduced to intolerable despair or Christian faith. Without accepting the necessity of either despair or Christian faith, Camus nevertheless fundamentally agrees with their analyses of the human condition. Malraux and Sartre do not argue for religious faith, but for an ethic of commitment and, in Malraux's case, an exalting heroism. Again, Camus does not share their conclusions, but even more powerfully sympathizes with their portrayal of human existence.

Among the other writers to whom Camus responded with sympathy are Franz Kafka, André Gide, and certain American novelists of the twenties and thirties. The reasons are as varied as the writers themselves. In Kafka he found a haunting vision of a meaningless world inhabited by people desperate for meaning. In Gide he found an example of the moral seriousness that has often characterized French writers; Gide had written prescient anticolonialist essays, had become a Communist in sympathy for the downtrodden, but had resigned from the party in protest after a visit to the Soviet Union. Gide also represented the highest ideals of French classical art, in which purity and simplicity are supreme aesthetic goals. One of Gide's best-known works is *L'Immoraliste* (*The Immoralist*), like *The Stranger* a brief first-person narrative, highly symmetrical in form, even set partly in Algeria; also like *The Stranger,* its hero's story is a sort of dispassionate confession, in which the stylistic clarity serves to bring out more forcefully the moral confusion and intellectual disorder of the narrator. Finally, many critics regard *The Stranger* as a stylistic imitation of Hemingway; the terse, factual sentences, presented almost without conjunctions or adverbs to link them, seem to convey in both writers a kind of exile's view of a chaotic world. But Camus was probably more deeply influenced by William Faulkner, whose southern Gothic imagination produced a world devoid of meaning that Camus found convincing and troubling.

In summary, Camus belongs to a tradition that includes existentialists, but he wanted to mark his distance from them. He thought of himself as a philosopher of the absurd. By "absurd" he meant the meaninglessness of existence, a perception similar to that of the existentialists, but Camus attempted to avoid what he regarded as their erroneous conclusion. That is, he tried to remain true to this vision of the absurd to the very end, and not to use it as the pretext for a leap of faith. He wanted to formulate a way of living within the absurd, or more accurately, he wanted to imagine life within the absurd. Ultimately, Camus was less a philosopher than a writer. His genius was not to have provided a philosophical analysis of the absurd, but to have created a fictional image of it.

Out of this background Camus produced a novel that won admiration both from a worldwide reading audience and from the tight Parisian intellectual circle that brought it to the public. By a remarkable set of strange twists, Nazi policy in France led the German occupiers actually to promote the survival of the most prestigious French publishing house, Gallimard. In the period between the two world wars, most of the great French writers and intellectuals were published by Gallimard and in many cases were employed in editorial capacities as well. They wrote regularly for a journal published by Gallimard, the *Nouvelle Revue Française,* which set literary standards for the French-speaking world. Gide was the most influential of the Gallimard circle. He and his colleagues instantly recognized the brilliance and originality of *The Stranger* when they read it in manuscript. They endorsed its immediate publication, and ensured that it would not pass unnoticed, despite the chaotic times.

Its bleak era had indeed produced a readership prepared for *The Stranger*'s stark message. The progress of Western civilization seemed to have brought only an increased capacity for self-destruction. Political ideologies had led to war, not to utopia; neither art nor religion nor philosophy had proved any deterrent to barbarism, violence, and all-out war. The individual could find no comfort outside himself or herself. For millions of people threatened with violent death either from persecution or from war, the question of whether life was worth living was urgent and difficult to answer; survival meant the sacrifice of all they had lived for. The philosophical absurd that Camus had meditated on in his studies became a familiar reality to most of the world. *The Stranger* takes up the question of the absurd and the value of life and provides, not a simple affirmative answer, but a guide for readers to think through the problem to their own solutions.

2
THE IMPORTANCE OF THE WORK

Camus's importance in the world of letters is perhaps most easily seen in his Nobel Prize award for literature in 1957. The prize committee called Camus an intellectual and moral leader who had "illuminated the problems of the human conscience in our times." Three decades later those words ring truer than ever, although in 1957 the choice of Camus came as a surprise and provoked controversy. He was the youngest person ever to win the prize, except for Rudyard Kipling fifty years earlier. He had produced a rather small body of works. In America some of the most influential critics regarded him as a pale copy of Sartre. Others had attacked him as a nihilist who believed that human life was absurd and futile; at best they treated him as an antiestablishment rebel.

In France, too, his reputation was shaky. He had obtained almost universal acclaim in the late 1940s, thanks to the success of *The Stranger, The Plague, The Myth of Sisyphus,* and his Resistance journalism for *Combat.* After the war Camus, Sartre, and many other French intellectuals appeared united in a common endeavor to rebuild France in the revolutionary tradition of liberty, equality, and fraternity. The exhilaration of the liberation soon faded, however, and unity collapsed before the terrible problems of postwar Europe. In 1951 Camus published his long essay *The Rebel,* which included a denunciation of the Communist party. Sartre allowed his journal to print a hostile review, after which Camus split with Sartre and many of his former associates of the left. In the 1950s France was torn asunder by the rising independence movement in Algeria, with its accompaniment of terrorism and repression. Camus, who was born and raised in French Algeria, refused to endorse either side without reservations, thereby further alienating his former friends. For several years, he published no new literature and his reputation declined as he grew more and more isolated trying to remain a moderate in a polarized debate.

Thus, in 1957, the Nobel Prize award shocked even the French. True, Camus had found his creative power again in 1956, when he published *The Fall,* a novel that some critics consider superior to *The Stranger.* But the committee had apparently recognized a fact that many literary authorities had missed: Camus was being read and admired by an enormous international public. Since its first printing of four thousand copies, *The Stranger* has sold four million copies in France and another three million in the United States. When the Nobel Prize finally focused attention on Camus, and brought him a certain respectability, critics close to a younger generation began to be heard. Thomas Molnar, writing for *Catholic World,* entitled an article "Albert Camus: Guide of a Generation," in which he asserted that "nine students out of ten, if asked to name a contemporary author with the greatest impact on youth, will mention Albert Camus in the first place" (272). Although we should allow for some hyperbole, this claim was substantially true, and was echoed and confirmed repeatedly in the press throughout the 1960s, both in the United States and in France. As Justin O'Brien and Leon S. Roudiez phrased it for the *Saturday Review* in 1960, he was "the spokesman of his generation and the conscience of his epoch" (19).

Their comment was, in fact, an obituary, for Camus's career was cut short by his death in an automobile accident in January 1960. No doubt this tragic end to some degree added to his prestige. A Camus-like character in *The Plague* describes his life as a desperate effort to be a saint without God. A reputation for saintliness burdened Camus in the 1950s; he knew he could not live up to it, and it angered both his enemies and his friends. His death, however, put him beyond reproach in a sense; he became a fallen hero. Since he could not be called on to take sides on the issues, he could be invoked by people with a broad range of political ideals. By 1968 Theodore Solatoroff observed wittily in the *New Republic* that Camus spoke from the grave almost every day "to confer some sort of nobility on other men's positions or prose" (27). It is true that the myth of Camus probably eclipses his works, but that in itself attests to the impact he had on the modern world.

Nevertheless, to rediscover the real Camus, it is essential to read his works, and for many *The Stranger* retains the full power of novelty and brilliance that it had in 1942. The noted American critic Alfred Kazin, reviewing a biography of Camus for the *New Republic* in 1982, calls *The Stranger* "his most famous and (I believe) still his best novel." Reflecting on Meursault's final moments, Kazin continues: "This is the Camus whom I tenderly remember for his opposition to capital punishment, for his opposition to every form of totalitarianism and every pretense behind it, for his premonitions, even at its height, that the Resistance spirit could not last" (34). *The Stranger* is a work of historical significance; it reveals a great deal about the Western mind in the middle of the twentieth century. But it is not only of historical interest; it shaped many of the ideas we hold today or, perhaps more accurately, it clearly articulated many of the questions we are still trying to resolve. To read *The Stranger* is to encounter one of the enduring literary masterpieces of the twentieth century, to relive a critical moment of our cultural heritage, and to engage in a living discourse on central moral issues of our times.

3

CRITICAL RECEPTION

The Stranger was published in 1942 in the middle of World War II. It was fortunate that the novel could appear at all during the German occupation, but its initial printing was small and it did not receive the circulation and public notice in print that it might have expected in peacetime. At the same time the troubled circumstances added glamour to a work that marked the first appearance of a previously unknown author, all the more when *The Stranger* was followed shortly by *The Myth of Sisyphus*. The first audience for *The Stranger* was made up primarily of Parisian literati, who saw it both as the work of a brilliantly original new talent and as a traditional French mixture of art and moral concern. *The Stranger* had no apparent relevance to contemporary political problems, but in a broader moral sense it explored the seemingly insoluble dilemma of the individual in an absurd universe and provided an antidote to nihilism and despair.

By the end of the war Camus had become famous and *The Stranger* was celebrated as a sort of underground masterpiece. Part of this fame derived from his work as a Resistance journalist. He had written a series of short essays, called *Lettres à un ami allemand* (*Letters to a German Friend*), published in various clandestine periodicals.

In 1943 he became a regular member and eventually the leader of the group publishing the clandestine newspaper *Combat*. In order to work on *Combat* he moved to Paris in 1943, served as an editorial reader for Gallimard, and lived in André Gide's apartment. He was thus in the very center of French intellectual and literary circles and circulated manuscripts of some of his works, especially his plays, which could not be performed during the occupation. He also met Jean-Paul Sartre, who was to emerge in the postwar years as the dominant figure among French writers and thinkers, and the two men became friends.

Sartre consecrated Camus's status as an author by publishing a long essay called "An Explication of *The Stranger*" in the periodical *Cahiers du Sud* in 1943, reprinted in *Situations I* in 1947. Sartre begins by recalling the excitement the book had caused but also some of the problems of understanding it. In particular, he notes, people wondered what Meursault stood for. Sartre then calls attention to the importance of *The Myth of Sisyphus* as a commentary on *The Stranger*, and defines Camus's concept of "the absurd" as "both a state of fact and the lucid awareness which certain people acquire of this state of fact." He explains, "chance, death, the irreducible pluralism of life and of truth, the unintelligibility of the real—all these are extremes of the absurd." Placing Camus in a tradition of thought starting with Pascal, Sartre remarks, however, that Camus is a passionate artist rather than a systematic philosopher. Awareness of the absurd comes as a brutal revelation into ordinary lives, not from rational deduction: "the absurd man will not commit suicide; he wants to live, without relinquishing any of his certainty, without a future, without hope, without illusion, and without resignation either." Most of this analysis is based on *The Myth of Sisyphus,* but Sartre says that Meursault is such a man, "one of those terrible innocents who shock society by not accepting the rules of its game."

Sartre maintains further that Camus did not write *The Stranger* to prove anything, but simply to portray. Writing a fiction is an act of humility, recognizing the limits of human reason, and, according to Sartre, Camus wants us to realize that there was no necessity for *The Stranger* to exist at all. It is "a leaf torn from a life" in the surrealists' image; it has the same value as any other act or object. Our understanding it depends on our accepting that it makes no effort to be understandable; it is just "there" for us, as the elements of Meursault's environment are there for him.

Sartre then takes up various themes in the novel: the meaninglessness of terms like *love*, the supremacy of the present moment, Meursault's lucidity, indifference, and silence. Sartre observes that the novel could have been appropriately titled *Translated from Silence*, and that Camus had to devise a new technique to "be silent with words." He largely discounts alleged similarities between Camus and Kafka, between Camus and American novelists, although he acknowledges that *The Stranger* uses a narrative style like Hemingway's. Sartre asks that we imagine a person in a telephone booth, observed from the outside so that we see the gestures but do not hear the conversation; such a person would appear absurd. Camus, he suggests, uses Meursault's mind as the glass partition through which the world is viewed. The technique makes the narrator a purely passive observer; it assumes that "any reality is reducible to a sum total of elements." Sartre points out that the method is valuable both for scientific analysis and for humor, but if it claims to give a full account of reality, the assumption is false, because "meanings are also part of the immediate data." In other words, it is impossible merely to observe; some signifying structure always determines what is observed.

Camus uses the device, Sartre then argues, to render the discontinuity of time. Each sentence simply asserts a new fact, without connection to what precedes and follows. Each one is a present moment, complete and potent while it lasts, but detached from any flow. Even the French verb tense contributes to this effect; rather than the vigorous narrative action conveyed in the simple past, the normal French literary past tense, Camus uses a compound past tense, which separates each action into an auxiliary verb, devoid of real meaning, and a past participle, the action expressed in static form. Dialogue is also suppressed, reported as indirect speech, lest it seem to have a special privilege as a moment of explanation and meaning. And, says Sartre, this discontinuity "enables Camus to think that in writing

The Stranger he remains silent." Paradoxically, however, the work it-self does not lack unity, quite the contrary; it is "a classical work, an orderly work, composed about the absurd and against the absurd."

Sartre's essay has had a powerful influence on subsequent criti-cism of *The Stranger*. He established the link between *The Stranger* and the ideas developed in *The Myth of Sisyphus,* he explained Meur-sault as an absurd figure, he related Camus's striking stylistic features to his themes, and he situated Camus in a line of morally committed French writers. Ironically, despite his citing Camus's idea that "if we are able to refuse the misleading aid of religion or of existential phi-losophies, we then possess certain basic, obvious facts," Sartre prob-ably also contributed to the myth of Camus as an existentialist, simply because of his own fame as the leading existentialist philosopher. And finally, linking Camus to the tradition of French moralists no doubt helped foster the myth of Camus the saint without God.

In 1946 *The Stranger* was translated into English, and Camus's reputation grew rapidly outside as well as inside France. New works continued to appear: journalism, essays, plays, and in 1947 *The Plague,* his second novel. After the publication of *The Rebel* in 1951, Camus parted company with Sartre and many of his former associates. Among a substantial and influential section of French intellectuals, especially the Marxists, his reputation declined in the early 1950s. Among the young, however, and outside France, he continued to be read and admired, as evidenced by his Nobel Prize in 1957. It is not surprising, however, that some of the most important new analyses of *The Stranger* came from abroad.

In 1955 Germaine Brée and Carlos Lynes, Jr., professors of French at two American universities, published a textbook edition of *The Stranger.* This in itself suggests how widely read the work was in America and England. Their introduction is intended to sum up criti-cal attitudes, rather than develop an original interpretation. On the whole, they still share Sartre's views of the novel, but their emphasis reveals a significant shift. On the one hand, they focus fresh attention on the ending, where Meursault's "adventure ends in a flash of in-sight." We realize he will "make his death itself an affirmation of the supreme value of life"; he "undergoes a kind of spiritual awakening." "If life were granted him he could begin to construct a new system of values and perhaps discover vital links between himself and other men." In short, at the ending he is elevated "to the stature of a lonely tragic figure" (9). Meursault, in their reading, is a more prestigious character and his fate offers more hope than in Sartre's. On the other hand, they blame society for much of Meursault's plight: "The anonymous, irresponsible procedure of society is much more criminal, in Camus's eyes, than the crime which it pretends to punish. Meursault is responsible for his act, of course, but he is also a victim—a victim of his own apathy and, in a more precise sense, of a society which has no values to offer him" (12).

In this reading *The Stranger* thus becomes in part a novel of social protest. The interpretation of Brée and Lynes took on added authority because Camus contributed a short foreword to their edition, in which he expressed similar ideas. He summarizes the story in the maxim "In our society any man who does not weep at his mother's funeral risks being sentenced to death" (vii). Meursault, he says, is condemned because "he does not play the game," which is to say, because "he refuses to lie." Camus suggests that we read *The Stranger* as the story of a man who is willing "to die for the truth," and he says he had tried to create in Meursault "the only Christ we deserve" (viii). Obviously, the comparison to Christ elevates Meursault to a very high level of prestige, and Camus also seems to concentrate on Meursault's treatment by society. Where Sartre had emphasized the philosophical idea of the absurd, Camus stresses society's hypocrisy and lies. In the years around 1960, Brée, Philip Thody, and John Cruickshank wrote influential books about Camus for English-speaking audiences; and while they have significant differences and express important nuances and reservations, they generally approach Meursault as a hero of the absurdist view.

At this point the idealization of Meursault had gone too far, and René Girard brought a much needed corrective in his article "Camus's Stranger Retried" in 1964. By that time, of course, Camus had been killed, and ideological or political biases tended less and less to obscure his status as a major writer. Camus was still hailed as a spiritual guide for the radical youth movements of the 1960s, but discussions of his literature no longer implied political positions. Girard argued that Camus's last novel, *The Fall*, published in 1956, could be read as a response to *The Stranger*, and was a greater work. In particular, Girard thought that Camus had come to recognize Meursault as more responsible than he implied in the 1955 foreword, and at the same time to have more sympathy for the lawyers and judges, since he realized that he was one himself. Girard writes, "Meursault is presented to us as completely indifferent to the collectivity, whereas the collectivity is supposed to be intensely concerned with his daily routine. This picture is false, and we all know it" (531). In fact, Girard believes, Meursault is desperate for attention, and even acknowledges it at the end by wishing for a large crowd to witness his execution. He represents a version of the "romantic self" (527), trying to escape solitude and mediocrity by claiming to will it, indulging pride by dramatizing self-abasement. In Girard's opinion, Meursault is "the portrait, or even the caricature, of a man Camus never was but swore to be, at the end of his adolescence, because he feared he could never be anyone else" (529).

Many readers today would say that Girard had also gone too far in attacking *The Stranger*, although much of what he says is right on the mark. In fact, many of his objections had been raised in the first reviews, but were forgotten in the general enthusiasm for the novel. Girard's critique did not consign *The Stranger* to oblivion, but rather prompted new readings, in part because most readers came to question many of Girard's assumptions. He accepts the necessity of reading the work as reflection of society, in order to argue that Camus falsified the portrait. But few critics today would attempt to relate the society depicted in *The Stranger* to the society any reader lives in, or ever lived in. When we talk about society in *The Stranger*, we are discussing at least a triple fiction: what we imagine Camus imagined Meursault would imagine. Likewise, Girard denies the validity of the standard moral interpretation, only to urge his own, derived more from *The Fall* than from *The Stranger*, but still taken to represent Camus's moral teaching. And finally, Girard draws arguments from assumptions about Camus's state of mind when he was writing *The Stranger,* but these assumptions are only other fictions, not facts.

At the same time as some critics were discovering new and disturbing aspects to the character of Meursault, others were turning their attention to Camus's art and narrative technique. For some "New Novelists," like Nathalie Sarraute and Alain Robbe-Grillet, *The Stranger* served as a model of an obsolescent tradition. Among academic critics Brian T. Fitch deserves special mention, because he has continued to write brilliantly on Camus and *The Stranger* for three decades. Spurred in part by Camus's fame as a Nobel laureate and by his untimely death in an accident in 1960, critics in the 1960s produced a large body of work on *The Stranger,* analyzing its style, its narrator, its themes, its structure, its images. In 1972 Fitch published a new book on *The Stranger,* with a selective bibliography of more than a hundred works discussing the novel; he devotes about half of his own book to summarizing the various interpretations under seven broad headings: biographical, political, sociological, metaphysical, existentialist, ontological, and psychoanalytical readings. Finding problems with all these methods, Fitch himself develops an interpretation based on textual analysis and the role of the reader.

The fallacies or unacknowledged premises in traditional methods of literary interpretation have been a central concern of literary theorists since the 1950s. Recent critical approaches to *The Stranger* have taken account of these structuralist and poststructuralist theories. Structuralist readings have highlighted patterns in order to relate the story to other patterns of meaning; we understand *The Stranger* not as the representation of something real and specific, but as the embodiment of a scheme of meaning already present in our minds, possibly as a genetic endowment, something like a computer's operating system. Related to these are mythic and psychoanalytical interpretations. In the former, Meursault's adventure is said to reenact a story embedded since prehistory in the human psyche; Meursault is a hapless innocent, caught up in the workings of fate, propelled toward the murder by divine forces acting through the sun and the sea. In the latter, Meursault is supposed to relive scenes from Camus's past, especially his oedipal lust for his mother and his jealous desire to kill and supplant his father.

Poststructuralist analyses have concentrated on the ways in which the text is about itself. Rather than connecting the reader to some new reality, the novel dramatizes the problems of representation, communication, and interpretation. Meursault's inability to give a convincing account of his actions is seen as a failure of language, not of the judicial system or the moral code of society. Moreover, language must fail; it can never capture a reality that is radically outside it, but can only refer constantly to other linguistic structures. Meursault is almost a preverbal man, whose actions follow so close on the sensual impulse that his motives are literally indescribable. But the murder ensnares him in the realm of language, and eventually he is compelled to verbalize his pure subjectivity.

Still other recent critics approach the novel from the perspective of the reader, arguing that whatever sense the story has is generated by the reading as much as by the text. *The Stranger* both depicts the act of reading, as when Meursault receives the telegram announcing his mother's death, and thematizes reading, as when the lawyers compare Meursault to a book that they then read and interpret for the jury. Such an approach can accommodate evolving interpretations brought about by historical change and conflicting interpretations caused by differences in viewpoint. If one reads as a woman or as an Arab, one will certainly react to Raymond differently from Meursault, and one's tendency to identify with Meursault or to cast him in a sympathetic role will thereby be reduced if not altogether stifled. *The Stranger* may nonetheless appear a brilliant depiction of the inherent problems in machismo and colonialism.

After almost fifty years *The Stranger* no longer evokes the feelings of surprise and strangeness that it did when it first appeared. Educated readers around the world have grown up with it, and Meursault is not such a stranger any more. Yet it seems to have lost little of its power and richness for latter-day readers. Changes in both moral sensibility and critical attitude have only led to the discovery of new complexity and new rewards in Camus's masterpiece.

A READING

4

INTRODUCTION

TRANSLATION PROBLEMS

Almost a half century has passed since Camus first published *L'Étranger*. It was immediately recognized as an important work of literature and seems solidly established by now as one of the master-pieces of French literature. As is usually the case with great works of art, it has been read and reread, interpreted and reinterpreted. Critics have discovered or invented depths of meaning and layers of symbol-ism. A work that seemed to express the despair and pessimism of the 1930s, 1940s, and 1950s, the years of the Great Depression, World War II, and the slow rebuilding of a shattered Europe, has also seemed to express the anxiety and doubt of the 1960s, 1970s, and 1980s, years of relative peace and prosperity but also of intellectual crisis about meaning and representation.

What the first readers noticed about *L'Étranger*, however, was its simplicity and directness. It hardly seemed to be literature, because its style was so plain, so natural, so ordinary—although, paradoxically, these qualities are anything but ordinary in literature. At least on the surface the novel is actually very easy to read and to understand; as a result, teachers have often chosen it as a text for French language classes in America and elsewhere and many foreigners know it in the original French. The English translation by Stuart Gilbert, published in 1946, has had a great effect in spreading Camus's fame. Since the present study is written in English and intended primarily for English-speaking readers, Camus's writings have been quoted throughout in English translation. The reliance on published translations poses certain problems, however, that need to be addressed right from the start.

Title. First of all, the title is exceedingly difficult to render well in English. The French word *étranger* means "foreigner" or "alien." A standard French dictionary, the Petit Robert, gives the following definitions: "Person whose nationality is not that of a given country; person who does not belong, or is considered not to belong, to a family or clan; person with whom one has nothing in common." For Camus, the last two meanings were certainly the most important, but in English "foreigner" and "alien" refer too specifically to questions of nationality and legal status. That unwanted emphasis would have been even more inevitable in the 1940s, because of the refugees and displaced persons after the war. In England the translation was entitled *The Outsider,* which captures the sense of the term reasonably well, while in America it has been known as *The Stranger,* which is further from the original meaning but retains a cognate form. Since the French *étranger* is very close to *étrange,* or "strange," that etymological kinship has some value. As there is no fully satisfactory solution, many English-speaking critics prefer to use the French title, even when referring to the translation for most other purposes. In this study the novel will be called *The Stranger,* but readers may wish to bear in mind the other possibilities. A title is, in some respects, a capsule interpretation, for it invites the reader to look at the work from a particular angle and suggests certain themes or focuses. In Camus's other works, the idea of a symbolic city—that is, a place where one is a citizen—plays a major part. The same image could very well be applied to Meursault, who is symbolically, if not literally, an alien.

Past Tenses. A second translation problem arises in almost every sentence. The French language uses a special tense for literary narration, called the *passé simple* or *passé défini*—literally, the "simple past" or "definite past." It derives from the Latin preterite, as in Julius Caesar's famous message "Veni, vidi, vici" (I came, I saw, I conquered; in French, *Je vins, je vis, je vainquis*). Until the last century, French speakers used the simple past in conversation and informal writing, but its use has been declining for centuries and by now it has died out in all uses except formal narrative. Every literate French speaker knows how to use the simple past, but in conversation and in informal writing (such as a letter), the French today use the *passé composé*—literally, the "compound past," but more accurately called the present perfect tense. In form it resembles the English present perfect—"I have come, I have seen, I have conquered": "Je suis venu, j'ai vu, j'ai vaincu." But in English the choice between the simple past and the present perfect tenses depends on the meaning, which differs subtly but perceptibly from one to the other, expressing two different relationships between the subject of the sentence and the time of the action. Both tenses can be used in all contexts, from the elevated style of high art to the casual banter of friendly conversation. In French, by contrast, the two forms usually have the same meaning, and only the writer's situation or level of discourse is different. This aspect of French style is difficult to explain and impossible to translate, because there is nothing comparable in English.

The essential point is that Camus wrote *The Stranger* in the *passé composé* where the *passé simple* was not simply normal but almost obligatory in a narrative of that sort. The result was to give Meursault's story a powerful immediacy, as if it were not literature at all, but truly the voice of an ordinary person speaking or the pages of a personal diary. Roland Barthes, one of the most important French literary critics of Camus's era, cited *The Stranger* as the first example of what he called "writing at the zero degree"—a "neutral" and "innocent" writing, "a sort of basic speech, equally far from living languages and from literary language proper," "a transparent form of speech," "almost an ideal absence of style," "a neutral and inert state of form," in other words, a language that gives the illusion of not being there at all, of letting the listener or reader go straight through the words to the reality they represent (Barthes 1984, 64). The consistent use of the *passé composé* helped to create that effect. There is no way whatsoever for an English translation to convey the quality of Camus's language, except to avoid literariness and elevated style as much as possible. Meursault speaks or writes most of the time in a natural colloquial manner, which in French is more sharply differentiated from literary style than in English.

Barthes, however, demonstrated that zero-degree writing was an illusion, created by a complex and subtle technique. One might say that the reader is taken off guard; the language sounds so natural that we fail to realize how the writer is actually organizing it so as to manipulate our reactions. Another early critic of *The Stranger*, Sartre, saw in these simple forms an attempt to do something very complex, to represent the alienation of the human consciousness in a world without meaning. In the *passé composé* the act represented by the verb is split in two, with the potentially active verb being reduced to an inert and timeless participle, while all the existential force of change in time is given to a meaningless auxiliary verb. In Sartre's view, even when Camus is apparently striving for the greatest simplicity, he chooses his words and his syntax to express more than what first appears. Patterns emerge, for example, that link parts of the novel to each other, and tie *The Stranger* to other works. Moreover, despite its predominantly matter-of-fact tone, there are passages in *The Stranger* that are full of poetic imagery and lyrical intensity.

Barthes's reasoning showed among other things that the world of *The Stranger* is composed entirely of words. Although we can see that Camus drew on real people, places, and events to construct his fictional world, these sources cannot be used to correct what he wrote or to determine its meaning. Even what Camus himself said about his purpose or original conception does not have more authority than the text of the novel, because these other statements can only be other texts. We interpret them, just as we interpret *The Stranger*. This is true whether we are considering a biography of Camus, a history of Algeria, a psychological study of murderers, an explanation of the French system of justice, or a foreword written by Camus himself. The closest anyone can ever get to the reality of *The Stranger* is its language. Since it was written in French, however, and we are discussing an English translation, a third problem arises for the critic.

English Translations. A translator can never exactly duplicate the qualities of a text in a new language; recall the proverb To Translate Is To Betray. We have seen, for example, how the *passé composé* and the title have no precise English equivalents. Literary texts, since they have been carefully crafted, intensify the difficulty. Obviously, readers of the English translation are not reading Camus's language but a text based on it, and this new text to some degree interprets the original, as when a choice must be made among *The Stranger, The Outsider, L'Étranger, The Foreigner,* or *The Alien* as a title. Each one would have different connotations and each one might require different choices elsewhere in the novel, so as to echo or avoid echoing the title. It is no doubt a sign of the novel's strength and depth of imagination that it has been as popular and as influential in translation as in the original; indeed, Camus may have been more consistently read and respected in America than in France.

One could reasonably argue that a study of the translated version should limit itself to the translation; the only text you can interpret is the one you have read, and if something has been lost in translation, is there any point in talking about it or trying to put it back? Furthermore, it is widely agreed nowadays that texts contain many meanings the author never intended to put there and that an author's intention matters very little anyway, in part because it is really unknowable. What an author says about his or her intention is just another text, subject to interpretation—it may be ironic, playful, deceitful, self-deluded, etc. One of the foremost scholarly critics of Camus, Brian T. Fitch, argues that even the title is irrelevant to a reading of the text, because it does not concern the text itself, but only the author's intentions about it.

While it is true that the whole reality of a literary work is contained within the text, it is equally true that readers bring their own storehouse of knowledge and experience to the process of interpretation. In general, the richer that storehouse, the quicker and more satisfying the understanding. A sophisticated English-speaking reader could get a lot out of *The Stranger* without knowing any French; even a relatively naive reader would probably find that reading *The Stranger* was enjoyable and profitable, because it is a very accessible novel. At the same time, however, the broader our cultural background, the faster we read, the better we understand, and the more we remember. One of the aims of this study is to provide background relevant to reading *The Stranger,* and the original French text is an important part of that background.

This study assumes, therefore, that the original French text retains a greater authority than the translation and is the point of departure for any study of *The Stranger.* Stuart Gilbert's 1946 English translation, which has sold millions of copies and remains the only available paperback edition, has been much criticized since the first reviews for its infidelity to the French original. Two American scholars, John Gale and Helen Sebba, have written articles pointing out the most glaring instances and analyzing the cumulative effects of the individual variations; readers who know at least a little French might want to look them up. In 1988 Matthew Ward published a new translation that follows Camus's language a great deal more closely and should supersede Gilbert's version. Quotations of *The Stranger* in this study are from Ward's translation, but since many readers may still be using the Gilbert text in paperback, page references are given to that edition as well, identified by the abbreviation "SG." Even so, it may prove difficult to locate some of the lines because the texts differ so extensively, a fact that serves to prove the point being made here about the problems of using a translation and the necessity of giving precedence to Camus's original French text.

GENERAL CHARACTERISTICS

In French or in English, *The Stranger* is relatively easy to read; the language is simple, the characters recognizable, the events mostly ordinary. It is set in Algiers, the principal city of Algeria, a nation on the

Introduction

North African coast; Camus was born and grew up there. When he wrote the novel, Algeria was considered part of France; it became independent in 1962, after several years of violence. Although Camus was deeply affected by the struggle for Algerian independence in the 1950s, and was concerned even in the 1930s by the misery of the Arab population, the political and social contexts play almost no part in the novel. What matters in the setting is the hot sun and the beach, an apartment house, a restaurant, a cinema, the street life of a working-class neighborhood, a courtroom, a prison, and in general the familiar institutions of a city in an economically and politically developed country.

Plot. It is generally assumed that the title refers to the main character, a young man who works as a clerk in a shipping company. His last name is Meursault; we never learn his first name. The story can be summarized thus:

In part 1, Meursault learns that his mother has died. He goes to the nursing home where she lived to attend her funeral. The next day he goes to the beach, meets Marie Cardona, a woman he used to know in his office, takes her to the movies, and sleeps with her. He spends a routine Sunday alone, and a routine week at work. A neighbor, Raymond Sintès, asks for his help in an unsavory affair with a Moorish woman; Meursault obliges by composing a letter to her. The two men thus become friends. When Raymond beats the woman a few days later, Meursault testifies on his behalf to the police. Raymond invites Meursault and Marie, who have become engaged, to a party at a friend's bungalow by the beach. The Moorish woman's brother and an Arab friend appear on the same beach. A confrontation occurs between the Arabs and the European men; the brother slashes Raymond's cheek. Then Meursault walks on the beach alone, unexpectedly comes on the Arab again, and shoots him.

In part 2, Meursault is tried for the murder. He talks to an examining magistrate and to his own lawyer in pretrial hearings. Marie visits him in prison and writes to him. He becomes accustomed to life as a prisoner. At the trial his friends prove inarticulate and ineffective as witnesses, but Meursault himself seems to lose interest in the proceedings and feels equally detached from the presentations of the prosecutor and of his own lawyer. The prosecutor emphasizes his behavior at his mother's funeral and in the days following, portraying it as callous and criminal. The jury condemns Meursault to be guillotined. In the final chapter he explodes in rage against the prison chaplain and then seems to find some kind of inner peace.

Narrator. It is important to know, in addition, that Meursault himself tells the story. He therefore interprets the events for us. In a brief summary the sequence is easy to follow, but it does not make much sense as a story. It is hard to see what the mother's funeral has to do with the murder of the Arab and why Meursault seems so indifferent to his trial and to his death sentence. We expect a storyteller to tell us not only what happened, but to some extent why it happened. What the storyteller leaves out, we tend to supply ourselves. For example, the following passage from the beginning of *The Stranger* describes a sequence of events: "The home is two kilometers from the village. I walked them. I wanted to see Maman right away. But the caretaker told me I had to see the director first. He was busy, so I waited a while. The caretaker talked the whole time and then I saw the director" (4; SG 2–3).

The first two sentences state facts, although of different sorts. The first is an external and permanent condition; its mention here implies that Meursault thought of it at this moment. The second is an event, which Meursault brought into existence by choosing to do it. Because of their placement, a reader tends to conclude that awareness of the distance somehow caused Meursault to walk to the home. Since nothing in this situation seems unusual, a commonsensical reader might gloss the lines by thinking: "Two kilometers is a relatively short distance for a healthy young man to walk, and so Meursault's walking probably indicates his preference rather than, for example, his poverty or the lack of other transportation."

Between those two sentences, however, one could insert an infinite number of explanatory phrases. The simplest would be either "and" or "but"; the former still suggests that walking is a reasonable choice, while the latter suggests that some other way would have been expected. The space might be used to hint that Meursault was mourning his mother: "and, as I had always done when I visited Mother, . . ." or "and, in order to collect my thoughts, . . ." Or it might be used to make Meursault seem indifferent: "and, as I was in no hurry, . . ." or "and, in order to delay my arrival. . . ." It could suggest fate working against him: "and, as there were no taxis. . . ."

Meursault, however, never tells his motives for walking, nor, continuing the passage, why he wanted to see his mother, any more than he tells why the director was not free or, in this passage anyway, what the caretaker chatted about. These are ordinary enough events so that we can imagine a score of plausible ways to answer such questions, should they occur to us. Since Meursault does not go into his motives, however, it is puzzling why he tells us as much as he does; it is hard to see what these trivial circumstances have to do with the principal event under way, the mother's funeral.

A few pages later Meursault finds himself in a room with his mother's coffin, and the caretaker offers to show him the body, but Meursault declines. The caretaker asks why not, and Meursault answers, "I don't know" (6; SG 6), making explicit and conscious the lack of motivation that is present throughout. Here again, we can imagine reasons, such as fatigue, or a reluctance to put the caretaker to the trouble of unscrewing the cover, or perhaps a certain queasiness because the caretaker had told him during their earlier chat that, owing to the heat, the body would have to be buried quickly. Meursault, however, does not explain his change of mind to the caretaker, nor does he explain it in retelling the incident, even though later in the story his indifference on this occasion serves as evidence against him. The next incident is the caretaker's remark that the nurse has an abscess; it has no apparent connection to what precedes or follows it, except chronological order. It is as if, for Meursault, such random elements in his surroundings are no different from the seemingly purposeful acts he performs. The way he tells his story, everything just happens. Furthermore, it is as if in telling the story, he has no sense of its main themes; he appears to note down details haphazardly, as if they all have equal importance.

In the novel Camus, through the voice of Meursault, provides a great deal of precise information about each of the major events. We follow Meursault through the funeral and the weeks following in considerable detail. Until the murder, at least, he does nothing unusual or dramatic enough to require much explanation; but then in retrospect we realize that we do not know much about his motives for any of his actions. As a result, most readers come away from the story with questions about several key moments: Why does Meursault shoot the Arab? Why does the trial go the way it does? Why does Meursault seem so indifferent, so detached, so much a stranger? Since these are the problems that strike readers first, they seem like a useful way to approach the novel.

CRITICAL METHODS

Thousands of pages have been written explaining *The Stranger,* in part or in whole. Some of the principal methods of explanation were cited in the chapter on critical reception. The approach adopted here is not systematic in the same way and could best be described as eclectic and humanistic. It attempts to respond to the questions that occur to educated but not expert readers, in terms that they might use themselves. It does not assume that literary criticism has a scientific method and it does not rely on any elaborated explanatory theory, such as existentialist philosophy, Marxist politics, or Freudian psychoanalysis. Insights drawn from these and other approaches may be cited where they seem relevant, but in lay terms and without footnotes to the source works. A great deal in this study, as in almost anything following on so many prior commentaries, is not original criticism or interpretation; ideas are mentioned and explored because they seem sound and illuminating, not because they are new. The source works are listed in the bibliography, but giving exact references for every idea that has been expressed on the subject would have encumbered this study enormously and worked against the readable tone it seeks. Insofar as possible, it strives to imitate a discussion among intelligent readers with varied backgrounds.

Most academic critics consider it inappropriate to discuss fictions as if the events and the characters were real. One of the best studies of *The Stranger*, however, Robert Champigny's *Pagan Hero*, actually does take a deliberate stance within the world of the novel as if it were real, but it is exceptional. Speculations, for example, over whether Meursault will win his appeal, an outcome not treated in the novel, would simply be dismissed as improper by most critics, although at least one has argued that the appeal has already been denied when Meursault writes. It is true that the question cannot be answered; the novel leaves Meursault perpetually suspended, with his lawyer having announced his plan to appeal, but with Meursault thinking mostly about his imminent execution. The fact that many readers ask the question reveals something about the novel's effect, however, and for that reason alone the question deserves to be taken seriously; a novel that readers confuse with reality raises different problems from one that maintains an obvious distance from the real. Moreover, without naively trying to determine what will "really" happen to Meursault, one can discuss the direction in which the novel seems to be moving; the fiction contains information that can be interpreted as pointing toward or away from a successful appeal, and the sense of its direction constitutes an important part of one's sense of its meaning. And finally, even a gratuitous assumption can be usefully scrutinized for its effect on the interpretation. For example, if we assume that Meursault will be spared the guillotine, how might we alter our view of him and of society, and thus our understanding of the novel?

Critics also frequently adopt a posture of refusing to consider anything not within the text of the novel. Some claim, for example that Camus's life and other works should not be used to explicate *The Stranger*, nor should the political situation in Algeria. This insistence on textual analysis has the merit of maintaining a common discourse among critics, and of preventing some flagrant misreadings. But it is difficult to regard it as a rigorous method, because to read even the simplest text requires applying a vast fund of externally acquired information. The first sentence of *The Stranger*—"Maman died today"—calls on a certain knowledge of family arrangements; it depends on our expectation of grief to generate some shock over its matter-of-fact tone and the odd continuation—"Or yesterday maybe, I don't know" (3; SG 1); the term "maman" rather than "my mother" we recognize as expressing intimacy, etc. In his translator's note Matthew Ward, citing Camus's notebooks and Sartre's criticism, explains that he chose the childish "Maman" over Gilbert's more adult "mother" to emphasize "the curious feeling the son has for his mother" (vii). Likewise, into our reading of this sentence will go everything we know about mothers, death, and mothers' deaths; if we know something of Camus's mother, there seems to be no compelling argument for ignoring that information, just as there is no reason to ignore the original French text.

The critical position that results is, to be sure, no freer of arbitrary assumptions and ideological biases than any other. The questions discussed in this study arose in specific settings, chiefly university classrooms in the United States, among students who were predominantly middle-class and liberal. This is not the place to defend our ideological presuppositions. It is enough to acknowledge that they exist and to make them explicit when they seem to impinge on the reading. The purpose is neither to present Camus as an adherent of our outlook, nor to impose our outlook on Camus. Rather, it is to acknowledge the appeal that *The Stranger* holds for us, to elucidate the reasons for it, and to examine the ways in which the novel involves us in interpreting it and in interpreting our own lives.

5

THE MURDER OF THE ARAB

Its Centrality

The murder of the Arab is clearly the central event of the novel. Camus placed it in fact right in the middle of the book. It is the last incident recounted in part 1, so its importance is underscored by a structural break in the story. It is related in one of the longer chapters, which records in fine detail the events of the day, even when their relevance is not obvious—for example, several paragraphs are devoted to describing how Marie and Meursault frolic in the sea. The murder marks an obvious change in Meursault's life, from free man to prisoner, and some more subtle associated changes, such as his increasing introspection and concern with memory. Meursault himself describes the shooting in terms that emphasize both the destruction of a past and the start of something new: "and there, in that noise, sharp and deafening at the same time, is where *it all started*. I shook off the sweat and the sun. I knew that *I had shattered the harmony of the day*, the exceptional silence of a beach where I'd been happy" (59, my italics; GS 76).

This violent crime also interrupts the routine flow of the story. Until the murder, nothing very dramatic has happened and nothing dramatic seems likely to happen. Partly, of course, this air of normality results from the way Meursault tells the story. His mother's death could have been a momentous event, but he begins the novel by saying about it: "Maman died today. Or yesterday maybe, I don't know" (3; GS 1). The matter-of-fact tone and the uncertainty combine to make us feel that this is not a significant event. In many stories the first moments of love seem portentous. Of his first night with Marie Meursault says, "Toward the end of the show, I gave her a kiss, but not a good one. She came back to my place. When I woke up, Marie had gone" (20–21; GS 24). One could hardly be farther from romantic rapture. A few days later Meursault agrees to marry Marie, and that too could have been presented as a turning point in his life; but he relates their engagement as if it were a routine decision: "That evening Marie came by to see me and asked me if I wanted to marry her. I said it didn't make any difference to me and that we could if she wanted to" (41; GS 52). Earlier the same day his boss offered him the opportunity to take a job in Paris, to which Meursault replied with similar indifference, "I said yes but that really it was all the same to me" (41; GS 52). The boss apparently regards this response as a refusal, so of course nothing more comes of it.

In literature it is often the case that a minor incident turns out to be the seed of an intense conflict or of vast complications. Once we know that Meursault's friendship with Raymond Sintès leads to the confrontation with the Arabs, and thus ultimately to the killing, the early scenes with Raymond seem ominous in retrospect. In their first scene together, Meursault agrees to write a letter luring Raymond's former mistress to a meeting where Raymond plans to beat her. Meursault tries his best to please Raymond, he says, because he "didn't have any reason not to please him" (32; GS 41). When Raymond beats the woman, Meursault does not call the police simply because he "didn't like cops" (36; GS 45). He even gives false testimony to the police on Raymond's behalf, but omits the scene from his primary account. Instead, as he, Marie, and Raymond set off for the fatal beach, he mentions casually that "the day before, we'd gone to the police station and I'd testified that the girl had cheated on Raymond" (48; GS 60). On close analysis, Raymond appears sinister and despicable, Meursault's relation to him appears dishonorable, and the narrative appears deliberately deceptive. On first reading, however, as Meursault presents the story, Raymond's activities seem no more significant than those of other friends and neighbors, like Emmanuel who hops a ride on a truck with Meursault, or old Salamano who mistreats but loves his dog, or Céleste who talks in clichés, or the robotlike woman who sits near Meursault in the restaurant. Any of them could supply the pretext for engaging Meursault in some dramatic adventure. By Meursault's account, however, until the murder, he and all these people lead humdrum lives, and nothing seems to predestine him to kill another human being.

RELATING THE MURDER

In narrating the murder scene itself, Meursault expresses very much the same attitude as he has previously; his actions have no conscious motives. The stage is set as if by accident, and that impression is reinforced by the accumulation of details. Meursault tells this day almost moment by moment. Raymond had issued the invitation in the preceding chapter. The day begins in Meursault's room, where he and Marie have spent another night together. He tells of his headache and a bitter taste in his mouth, of Marie's white dress and Raymond's blue trousers, of their decision to take a bus rather than walk. Some of the details have symbolic functions. Marie remarks that he has a "funeral face" (47; GS 60), alluding both to the funeral and to the impending murder. When they first go out, the sun hits Meursault "like a slap in the face" (47; GS 60)—an early hint of the sun's coercive role and of Meursault's taking Raymond's place, for Raymond had been slapped earlier by a policeman. They bang on Raymond's door to summon him, foreshadowing the gunshot raps "on the door of unhappiness" at the time of the murder. More direct signs of trouble emerge, too. Meursault recalls that he had testified for Raymond the night before, and they see the Moorish woman's brother with some friends, apparently stalking them.

For the moment, however, the Arabs do not follow the trio, and Meursault recounts an idyllic morning at the beach. He describes the setting, and step by step he relates their arrival at the bus stop, their walk across the plateau, and their meeting with the Massons, who own the bungalow. Masson, Marie, and Meursault decide to go for a swim; Meursault recalls the conversation, their games in the water, and their sunbathing. Then they return to the bungalow for lunch; they have fish, meat, fried potatoes, bread, wine, and coffee. After lunch, Marie and Masson's wife do the dishes, while the three men go out for a walk. Nothing could be more ordinary than most of this morning, yet it takes up almost half the chapter.

Even knowing what is to come, one can find only ambiguous indications that this day is different from the others. Seeing Marie with Masson's wife, Meursault says, "*For the first time*, maybe, I really thought I was going to get married" (50, my italics; GS 63). It is a slim pretext, but one might argue that Meursault was becoming aware of a change in himself, away from his solitude and carefree irresponsibility, toward a family commitment. Indeed, later, he makes the fatal decision to return to the beach because of a vague reluctance to rejoin the women. In his glimpse of domestic life he may have felt an obscure threat to his freedom. The rest of the novel, in which he is imprisoned, shows his growing understanding of freedom and its value.

Throughout the novel Meursault sleeps while important events are occurring. He has difficulty waking up on the morning of the murder, he naps again on the beach, and he feels drowsy after lunch. The most common interpretation is that Meursault's torpor leads to his undoing—he shoots the Arab in a moral sleep, so to speak. One might argue, however, that this day develops differently, and that Meursault gets into trouble by being forced out of his somnolence. Marie awakens him in the morning, and again for lunch. Masson says that his wife always takes a siesta after lunch, whereas he prefers a walk; and so the men go out to walk on the beach, Meursault included, of course. Just as he gains a new insight into freedom, so too he comes to realize that he has been morally sleeping and to appreciate the value of life in opposition to the eternal sleep of death.

CONFRONTATIONS

Despite these possible clues that Meursault is changing even before the shooting, the impression that this is just another day dominates the first part of this chapter, right up to the first confrontation with the Arabs. There are three confrontations. In the first, Meursault, Masson, and Raymond are all three present. Raymond sees and recognizes his mistress's brother, with a second Arab man. All five men continue walking toward each other. Masson wonders aloud "how they'd managed to follow us all this way," and Meursault thinks that "they must have seen us get on the bus with a beach bag" (53; GS 67). In fact, nothing suggests very strongly that the Arabs really were tracking Raymond. The beach was virtually deserted in the midday heat, so that the chances of finding him were remote. Moreover, the Arabs hold the stronger position in this encounter, because one of them has a knife, but they do not attack with it, and abandon the fight rather than press their advantage. They do nothing to avoid the confrontation, it is true, but Raymond becomes the aggressor by going "right up to his man." Meursault cannot hear what is said, but interprets the Arab's gesture as an attempt to butt Raymond; it is Raymond, nonetheless, who lands the first blow. Masson then knocks the second Arab down with two quick punches. Raymond meanwhile has bloodied his adversary's face and is preparing to do worse; only then does the Arab produce his knife, with which he slashes Raymond's hand and face. Holding the three Frenchmen at bay with the knife, the two Arabs back off and flee.

Meursault's role in this initial fracas is very passive. He accepts the task assigned to him by Raymond, to stand by to help "if another one shows up" (53; GS 68). As in earlier episodes, Raymond calls on Meursault to witness his virile exploits, prematurely in this case, since the Arab pulls the knife just as Raymond brags, "Watch this. I'm gonna let him have it now" (54; GS 68). Meursault tries to shout a warning, but too late. In the aftermath the three men return to the bungalow, and Masson then takes Raymond to a doctor, leaving Meursault, as he puts it, "to explain to the women what had happened. I didn't like having to explain to them, so I just shut up, smoked a cigarette, and looked at the sea" (54; GS 69). As usual, he gives no clue as to the content of his thoughts, and nothing is reported of his conversation with the two women.

As the events soon show, however, he is much more assertive henceforth. His failure to join in the fight and his role of staying with the women show him for the first time excluded from the society he regards as his own. He had experienced some sense of isolation at Marengo, but his exclusion there does not trouble him as much as his low status in this incident; the funeral was, after all, an unfamiliar ceremony at which he was legitimately an outsider, whereas with Masson and Raymond he ought to feel fully one of the group. Even though Meursault presents himself as taciturn and inarticulate, he seems otherwise to Raymond, who uses him as a spokesman, both to write a letter to his mistress, to explain matters to the women, and to testify to the police. That world of words seems to Meursault a feminine realm, however, and he wants to belong to the masculine world of deeds. Up to this point in the novel nothing has roused Meursault from his lethargy; now, without his realizing it, what appears to be an obscure sense of male rivalry with Raymond is about to push him into uncharacteristic action. While he admits to no jealousy or anxiety, it is not irrelevant that Meursault noticed Raymond's effort to flirt with Marie earlier in the day. Raymond's belligerence and swagger are even more obvious efforts to seek validation from Meursault; in asking Meursault's opinion about the Moorish woman and about his conduct with the policeman, in offering Meursault a visit to a prostitute, as well as in calling on him to witness the fight with the Arab, Raymond both casts Meursault as a certain type of man, what we would call macho today, and challenges Meursault to live up to the role.

Masson and Raymond return from the doctor at one thirty, two hours after the first walk began. Raymond is in a surly mood and eventually announces that he is "going down to the beach . . . to get some air" (55; GS 70). Masson and Meursault both propose to go with him, but he tells them to mind their own business. Masson complies, but not Meursault: "I followed him anyway" (55; GS 70). This is Meursault's first rejection of authority, almost his first willful act in the novel. As usual, of course, he reveals nothing about his motives. The two men walk for a long time, apparently in silence. Meursault "had the impression that Raymond knew where he was going"; in one of the rare instances where he allows us to see his position as narrator who already knows the outcome, he adds, "but I was probably wrong" (55; GS 70). The reader may find his original view more probable; Raymond seems to be looking for the two Arabs and to know where to find them.

Whether or not Raymond knows where he is going, he and Meursault come upon the two Arabs by a stream near a large rock. The description becomes more and more lyrical and mythical from this point. The sun has grown unbearably fierce. The Arabs are lying peacefully by the stream, one of them playing three notes on a reed flute. Except for the three notes and the tinkling water, there is total silence and stillness. The scene is like a pastoral painting, defying time, change, and death. Yet into this timeless sanctuary Raymond has brought a revolver, and he once more plays the tough guy for Meursault: "Should I let him have it?" (56; GS 71).

In previous situations Meursault has more or less dodged such questions, acknowledging Raymond's feeling, but not committing himself. When Raymond first tells him the story of the unfaithful mistress, for example, Meursault responds with lines like, "I said you can't ever be sure, but I understood his wanting to punish her" (32; GS 40). This time, however, he takes control, and tells Raymond it would be "pretty lousy" to shoot the Arab before any words had been exchanged. Raymond immediately proposes to provoke the Arab with an insult, but Meursault counters again, "if he doesn't draw his knife, you can't shoot" (56; GS 71). Raymond has no further response, but Meursault concludes that he has "started to get worked up" and so he gives Raymond one more piece of advice: "Take him on man to man and give me your gun. If the other one moves in, or if he draws his knife, I'll let him have it" (56; GS 72). As Raymond hands over the gun, "we just stood there motionless, as if everything had closed in around us." In this strange suspended state Meursault's indifference takes on alarming proportions: "I realized that you could either shoot or not shoot" (56; GS 72).

As in the first encounter, the Arabs flee, slipping suddenly behind the rock. Meursault and Raymond return once more to the bungalow, and Raymond seems satisfied. But Meursault halts at the bottom of the stairs, unable, he says, "to face the effort it would take to climb the wooden staircase and face the women again" (57; GS 72). For Meursault time is still frozen in the moment of the encounter, under the pervasive glare of the sun. The heat thudding in his head makes it as painful to remain on the stairs as to go up. As before, Meursault is conscious of no reason to choose: "To stay, or to go, it amounted to the same thing" (57; GS 73). Nevertheless, he goes back to the beach and starts walking back toward the site of the last encounter.

Meursault relates the moment as if he never makes the decision. He drifts into an action because it is the easiest choice. To enter the cabin requires an effort, to remain on the steps causes pain. This explanation is not fully convincing, however, because walking on the beach also requires effort and leads to pain, but there, he says, "I gritted my teeth, clenched my fists in my trouser pockets, and strained every nerve in order to overcome the sun and the thick drunkenness it was spilling over me. With every blade of light that flashed off the sand, from a bleached shell or piece of broken glass, my jaws tightened. I walked for a long time" (57; GS 73). Eventually, he sees the rocks and remembers the cool spring where the second confrontation had taken place. Then, and only then, the cool water becomes obsessively important to him, and even then he has not thought of the Arabs again.

If this were a real event—if we were reading this story in a recent newspaper, or hearing it on a newscast—we would not accept this account. We would suppose that Meursault was concealing something, perhaps even from himself. In the second half of *The Stranger*, lawyers, judges, members of the jury, reporters, and a chaplain react in just that way. It is important to recognize, however, that Meursault, the only person who was there, the only person who could know, refuses to acknowledge any motive whatsoever for his return to the beach alone. It was the line of least resistance under the circumstances. He was living as he always had, caught up in the present moment, doing what seemed most comfortable at the time.

The Murder

Only when he comes close to the rocks and the stream does he realize that one of the Arabs is still there; in fact, he claims he had forgotten about the earlier incidents. Then, for a long time the two men stand facing each other without doing anything. Meursault is not so passive that he fails to recognize his freedom to choose what to do. He knows that he could have avoided the third confrontation; he even knew it at the time: "It occurred to me that all I had to do was turn around and that would be the end of it. But the whole beach, throbbing in the sun, was pressing on my back. I took a few steps toward the spring" (58; GS 74–75). His freedom serves no purpose, however, because he has no purpose himself. All his actions seem to him to well up spontaneously from nature. When the Arab first puts his hand in the pocket where the knife is, Meursault reacts as if by reflex: "Naturally, I gripped Raymond's gun inside my jacket" (58; GS 74). Why is that natural, since Meursault is not accustomed to carrying a gun? Only because he does it without thinking.

And then he takes one final, fatal step: "It was this burning, which I couldn't stand anymore, that made me move forward. I knew that it was stupid, that I wouldn't get the sun off me by stepping forward. But I took a step, one step, forward. And this time, without getting up, the Arab drew his knife and held it up to me in the sun" (59; GS 75). As before, Meursault knows that his action makes no sense; as in the previous instance, he knew it at the time, to the extent that he thought about it. But he did not think; he took one more step, in a series that goes back not just to the bungalow, but to the beginning of the book, for that is how Meursault has lived his life, acting by reflex rather than by reflection.

The instant of the murder has arrived. Aware, at least in

41

retrospect, of the significance of this action, Meursault relates it at length. Even here, however, he has almost nothing to say about his own thoughts and ideas: "All I could feel were the cymbals of sunlight crashing on my forehead and, indistinctly, the dazzling spear flying up from the knife in front of me" (59; GS 76). What he talks about is external—the sweat dropping from his eyebrows, the gleam of the knife, the glare of the sun, the hot wind off the sea. When he actually pulls the trigger, he phrases the sentence so that he himself disappears: "The trigger gave" (59; GS 76).

ABSENCE OF MOTIVE

After the shot, his perspective changes abruptly. He recognizes, first of all, that a momentous event has occurred: "there, in that noise, sharp and deafening at the same time, is where it all started" (59; GS 76). Unlike his mother's death or his betrothal to Marie, this deed marks a turning point. Curiously, he regards it as a beginning rather than an end, even though he has lost his freedom and, as he puts it, "shattered the harmony of the day, the exceptional silence of a beach where I'd been happy" (59; GS 76). Furthermore, he reestablishes himself in the active role: "Then I fired four more times at the motionless body where the bullets lodged without leaving a trace" (59; GS 76). Meursault offers no more explanation for the additional shots, in terms of motive, than for any of his previous actions. The act itself still belongs to his habitual pattern of behavior—impulsive, instinctive, unconscious. For the first time, though, he adds a prospective comment. This act will have consequences for the future. "And it was like knocking four quick times on the door of unhappiness" (59; GS 76).

It is easy enough to imagine reasons for Meursault's behavior. It seems probable that his macho attitude and unacknowledged rivalry with Raymond enter into it. He has for the first time really thought about being married; he reacts by rejecting both the company of women and whatever might be thought feminine in himself: fear, pity, conciliation, even passivity, which had been his dominant trait. On the first sally he recognizes that Raymond and Masson are old friends who form a pair from which he is excluded. His isolation is exacerbated when Raymond consigns him to an onlooker's role in the first fight, and still more when he is obliged to wait with Marie and Masson's wife while the other two men go to the doctor. He then outdoes Raymond both in sullen stubbornness and in aggressiveness. In the second trip to the beach Meursault replaces Raymond as the dominant male. He must make the third trip to vindicate his honor.

One critic has argued that Meursault was suffering from sunstroke. One could also mention that he has drunk a good deal of wine. There are ingenious psychoanalytical theories linking the Arab to Meursault's father, and political interpretations stressing the implicit racial tensions. Readers often discuss ways to defend Meursault in court, such as temporary insanity, or a plea of self-defense—after all, the Arab drew his knife first. Raymond escapes any blame, not only in Meursault's retelling but also in court; yet he provoked the quarrel with the Arab and drew Meursault into it.

The point of this crime, however, is that it has no purpose and no excuse. Other critics have emphasized that, whatever excuses one might make for the first shot, the other four shots remain to be accounted for. In part 2 the examining magistrate tries to press Meursault on the point, and he just falls silent, both at the time of his interrogation, and in recounting it. Some highly ingenious symbolic interpretations have been proposed: the dead Arab represents some hated figure, such as Meursault's father; once dead, the Arab really is Meursault's enemy, the evidence of his crime, and thus provokes his rage; the Arab is a symbol of death itself; the four shots signify time, history, the law, and the written word, as opposed to the three notes of the flute, signifying timeless harmony with nature; the murder is described in erotic terms and the four shots suggest an orgasmic rhythm.

Meursault's originality as a character is precisely that he has no interest in telling a story that explains his crime, either to make it forgivable or to make it comprehensible, whether we forgive it or not.

His very obtuseness is a sort of male trait; explaining things is associated with tearful women, silence with active men. It is hard to know whether Camus understood Meursault this way or not. Some of his remarks suggest that he believed Meursault to be a natural man, true to his most basic instincts, revolted only by pretense and hypocrisy. Meursault, however, is no more natural than anyone else; he is a recognizable product of socialization as a white working-class Algerian male. His refusal of introspection allows him to confuse his conditioned reflexes with instincts. His rejection of purposes and meanings makes him blind to his own motives. He genuinely does not know why he killed the Arab, for the same reasons that he does not know why he did anything else, either: every attempt to make him examine his motives he brushes aside as being either female entanglement or authoritarian oppression. If he cannot fall asleep, he falls silent; if he cannot withdraw physically, he withdraws mentally.

Despite Meursault's strange ordinariness and the odd banality of his life, part 1 ends at a familiar literary moment. A dramatic and mysterious event has erupted in the midst of the commonplace. The mystery is, of course, not who did it, but why it was done. Most readers would expect the story to proceed now toward an explanation of Meursault's motives. Searching his own soul, he should find a key to his behavior. Our usual expectations in reading a novel about a murder are going to be frustrated, however, although we are not meant to realize that yet. That key simply does not exist, but Camus will use our desire to find it to lead to a different sort of understanding. In life the judicial process bears the burden of assessing motives and assigning responsibilities; the court in *The Stranger* tries to perform that function. Most of the second half of *The Stranger* is taken up with Meursault's trial. We look at it next.

6

THE TRIAL

LITERARY TRIALS

The murder propels Meursault into the French judicial system. The five chapters of part 2 take up different stages of the trial: first his pretrial examination by a magistrate, then his adaptation to prison life, the trial itself, the verdict, and finally a chaplain's visit as he awaits execution. Courtroom scenes are a staple in literature; Camus greatly admired Stendhal's *The Red and the Black,* Dostoyevski's *Crime and Punishment,* Kafka's *Trial,* and Faulkner's *Requiem for a Nun,* in all of which courtroom judgments and legal procedures play a climactic role. The reasons that courtrooms make dramatic settings are easy to see. First of all, intense human passions conflict with each other. Second, in order to resolve the conflict the court must distinguish appearance from reality according to principles generally accepted by society. Since literature often explores the contrast between appearance and reality, the courtroom scene may serve as the test where society's perceptions are opposed to the author's. Third, even when basic agreement is reached on what really happened, the freedom of the individual often confronts the necessity for order and regulation; this too is a common theme in fiction. Fourth, complicated and ambiguous realities must be reduced to a simple distinction between guilty and not guilty; this inevitable oversimplification makes a striking counterpoint to the artist's ability to preserve the full complexity of the real. Finally, court decisions translate abstract ideas into practical consequences.

A trial takes place in a highly structured form, not unlike a work of literature. In both the observer has foreknowledge to some extent about what will come next, because it is dictated by generic conventions or by legal procedures. The content, nevertheless, may harbor surprises, and in fictional trials at least, the author depends on building up expectations and then not realizing them in the normal way. Finally, the rules of law reflect current social responses to such difficult questions as what is a fact, what is acceptable as evidence, what constitutes a valid argument, what is a proof. These questions are, of course, central to literature, too. Novelists have much more leeway than lawyers, judges, and juries; the courtroom is therefore often confined to the role of a rigid and constrictive social reality, while the novelist opens the reader's mind to a broader and richer understanding of life.

In many trials there are unexpected twists in the testimony, and there is usually suspense about the outcome. If there is a surprise in *The Stranger,* it is the literary one that there are no dramatic revelations, that the defendant's interest in his own case dwindles, and that the verdict comes as an anticlimax. The guilty verdict seems inevitable, since Meursault admits to the shooting and says almost nothing in his own defense. His own lawyer repeats the confession and emphasizes "extenuating circumstances" (105; GS 132). The death sentence is excessively harsh, to be sure, but Meursault's own boredom and detachment make it hard for the reader to feel deeply distressed. He reports the sentence in the same dismissive tone that he had used for his mother's death and his engagement to Marie: "the presiding judge told me in bizarre language that I was to have my head cut off in a public square in the name of the French people" (107; GS 135). Soon afterward the judge offers him the chance to say something, and he declines, as so often before; as usual, he tells the reader little more than he told the court. In part 1 of the novel we have a straightforward and full account of the murder and the events that precede it. Meursault is the only person who knows anything about this crime and he has no secrets to reveal; from his perspective, as we have seen, the events just happened.

That explanation, however, cannot satisfy the judicial system. Somehow a meaningful version of the events must be produced. The second half of *The Stranger* shows how the meaning is sought or, more accurately, created. In the simplest terms, each of the important figures in the case—the prosecutor, the defense attorney, Meursault himself— proposes an interpretation; the jury and the judge have the official responsibility to weigh the competing interpretations and validate one of them. The examining magistrate, the reporters, and the chaplain also propose interpretations, reflecting a broader social function. Ul- timately, we the readers also become caught up in the process of interpreting.

IMPLAUSIBILITY OF THE TRIAL

It is important to recognize from the outset that Meursault's trial, al- though Camus adopts many features from real tribunals and from lit- erary precedents, is not a credible judicial proceeding. Whatever Camus really thought of French justice, he made little effort to portray it realistically in *The Stranger*. The court is rather a symbolic distor- tion, a nightmarish mechanism viewed from its victim's perspective. It is appropriate to compare Camus to Kafka in this regard; Kafka strad- dles the border between reality and fantasy as a way of conveying the character's sense of an alien world. In "In the Penal Colony" a ma- chine literally inscribes guilt onto the prisoner's body; in "The Meta- morphosis" a man is transformed into an insect; in *The Trial* the accused cannot learn the charges against him. Unlike Kafka, Camus avoids flagrant violations of verisimilitude; nothing in *The Stranger* breaks the laws of nature, nothing resembles a miracle, nothing re- quires belief in the supernatural, nothing seems more appropriate to science fiction or fantasy genres. At the same time, the trial does not seem to be in complete congruence with the judicial institutions and social customs of its place and time.

One could perhaps attribute the trial's implausibility to the fact that Meursault is an unreliable narrator. Unreliable narration is a common fictional technique, which requires the reader to pay heed to the narrator's perception of reality, not to the reality itself. Usually the "reality" is only implicit and approximate, inferred by the reader from what the narrator says, corrected by a general sense of what is plausible and what is known of the narrator's biases. It can hardly be doubted that Meursault provides a highly unreliable account of his trial—he admits that his attention wavers, that his memory is selective, that his own concerns differ from those of the court. It is also obvious to most readers that the point of the novel does indeed involve Meursault's perceptions, and that Camus intended them to be applicable to a world the reader would recognize as real. Nonetheless it seems impossible to filter out or reconstruct a perfectly plausible trial from Meursault's unreliable narration. The distortions do not reveal a pattern with which we can explain Meursault, and the trial's implausibility stems less from unbelievable assertions than from inexplicable omissions.

There is a hiatus of a week between the end of part 1 and the beginning of part 2. Meursault does not say what happened after the shooting. Did he return to the bungalow? Did he run away? Did he get rid of the gun? Did the shots attract attention? Did the second Arab go for the police? Even presented as purely factual notations, in Meursault's usual laconic style, the answers to these questions would be relevant to a search for a motive; yet neither the prosecution nor the defense ever mentions Meursault's behavior after the shooting. The policeman who arrested Meursault and took evidence from the scene of the crime is never mentioned either, and apparently never called as a witness. Nor does the second Arab testify.

Masson takes the stand, apparently only as a character witness—an odd fact in itself, since he had barely met Meursault—for he does not recount the first brawl with the Arabs, in which he had taken part and in which the murder victim had pulled a knife and slashed Raymond. Marie gives testimony about her relations with Meursault, but not about seeing the Arabs the morning of the killing. Raymond makes some pertinent statements about the quarrel leading up to the fight, but there is no indication he is questioned about the gun, which belonged to him, or about the second encounter with the Arabs, when Meursault took the gun from him. In short, the trial is arranged so that it fails to bring out any facts about the killing except the ones presented in part 1, and it fails either to support or contradict those facts. Moreover, it neglects many clearly relevant and independently verifiable facts. Everyone colludes in focusing on Meursault's soul, especially Meursault himself.

INTERPRETATIONS OF THE KILLING

Prosecutor. The prosecutor occupies much the largest place in Meursault's account of the trial. His goal is to portray Meursault as a cold-blooded killer, who planned and executed the murder of the Arab. He calls to the stand Thomas Pérez, the director, and the caretaker from the Marengo nursing home to attest to Meursault's callousness. In reply to a defense objection of irrelevance, the prosecutor explains his logic, "I accuse this man of burying his mother with crime in his heart" (96; GS 122). The other witnesses all seem to have been summoned by the defense. Céleste, Masson, and Salamano make almost no impression. Marie's truthful testimony appears to substantiate the charge of callousness. The contemptible and obnoxious Raymond offends the court by his presumptuous air. While he tells the truth, he does Meursault little good by proclaiming their friendship; moreover, he brashly explains everything suspect or incriminating as the result of chance, inviting the prosecutor's ironic reply that "chance already had a lot of misdeeds on its conscience in this case" (95; GS 120). Chance is certainly a less persuasive explanation than the prosecutor's hypothesis that the murder was "to settle an affair of unspeakable vice" (96; GS 121).

When the prosecutor delivers his summation, even Meursault concedes that "what he was saying was plausible" (99; GS 125). Except for the allegation that Meursault provoked the brawl on the beach, nothing he says really contradicts the version Meursault gives in part 1. He concludes, however, that Meursault is too intelligent to have "acted without realizing what he was doing" (100; GS 126), although that is precisely what Meursault claims to be true. Ironically, the prosecutor implies that Meursault's claim is true in most cases: "this is no *ordinary* murder, no thoughtless act for which you might find mitigating circumstances" (100, my italics; GS 126). That fits Meursault's crime exactly: it was a thoughtless act, and therefore a very ordinary act of homicide. In social and moral terms, however, it is utterly unsatisfactory to let chance or impulse stand as the whole explanation. The prosecutor appeals to the almost universal human preference for meaningful interpretation over the concept of accident and chance. The jury agrees and even Meursault seems half convinced.

The prosecutor goes still further, however, and calls Meursault "an abyss threatening to swallow up society" (101; GS 127). His callousness proves his lack of a soul, or of any moral qualities whatsoever. In the prosecutor's harangue Meursault is described as a total alien, something less than human. By this reasoning he is guilty even of a crime he did not commit, the parricide that will be the next case on the docket. Meursault "paved the way" and "legitimized" the second crime (102; GS 128). No doubt the prosecutor exaggerates Meursault's public impact and the monstrousness of his crime, all the more because we presumably accept Meursault's account in part 1 as the true account of what really happened. The prosecutor errs in degree but not in principle, however; from society's point of view, the meaning of an action depends on its relation to established rules and on its function as a precedent. Meursault himself (although unconsciously) interprets and judges in precisely the same manner, understanding actions within a context of human conventions, as in the scene where he tells Raymond it would be unfair to shoot the Arab unprovoked. But Meursault's rules are different, his precedents other, and his concern for maintaining the system's coherence is not great.

Defense. Meursault's lawyer begins with several handicaps. He is appointed by the court, not hired by Meursault, and in the defendant's judgment at least, he is by no means as clever as the prosecutor. Moreover, Meursault does not cooperate with him. Early on, he warns that the prosecution is building a case based on Meursault's moral and emotional callousness. To counter it he tries to get Meursault to express grief, to which Meursault responds as he often did in part 1, "I probably did love Maman, but that didn't mean anything" (65; GS 80). For the lawyer's purposes, Meursault's responses are worse than inadequate, they sound like proofs of callousness; so he suggests a second interpretation: "He asked me if he could say that that day I had held back my natural feelings" (65; GS 80). Meursault simply says, "No, because it's not true." The lawyer can do no more than implore his client not to repeat these comments. Meursault resists in similar fashion any display of regret for the killing, telling the magistrate, "more than sorry I felt kind of annoyed" (70; GS 87), and conceding silently during the prosecutor's summation, "Of course, I couldn't help admitting that he was right. I didn't feel much remorse for what I'd done" (100; GS 126). The defense lawyer claims nonetheless that Meursault is "already suffering the most agonizing of punishments—eternal remorse" (105; GS 132), but Meursault has given him no basis for the assertion.

The lawyer's line of defense consists of an admission of the murder, with the allegation of attenuating circumstances. His summation presents Meursault as an "honest, hard-working man" who "had lost control of himself for one moment" (105; GS 132). We have noted his inept failure to bring up self-defense as an attenuating circumstance, but the fault is Meursault's as much as the lawyer's. Asked by the prosecutor why he had taken the revolver with him, Meursault says, "it just happened that way" (88; GS 110), mentioning neither the way in which he actually obtained the gun to prevent Raymond from using it, nor the plausible excuse that he feared the Arab's knife. In fact, Meursault glosses over whatever the lawyer does say on the subject with the remark, "He rushed through a plea of provocation" (103; GS 131). Throughout the trial Meursault works at cross-purposes with his lawyer; when the lawyer obtains the caretaker's admission that he, too, smoked at the funeral, Meursault breaks his usual silence to confess having offered the cigarette. When the lawyer tries to minimize the effect of Thomas Pérez's testimony, Meursault faults him for questioning in "an exaggerated tone of voice" (91; GS 114). When the odious Raymond claims Meursault's friendship, Meursault, although apparently taken aback, confirms it. To sum up, Meursault regards his lawyer as "ridiculous" and "a lot less talented than the prosecutor" (103–104; GS 131).

Quite consistently, Meursault obstructs the development of a defense interpretation of the crime. He denies statements that construe his feelings and attitudes in exculpating ways, he keeps silent about verifiable facts that tend to excuse him, he talks to the magistrate without consulting his lawyer, and he even tends to cooperate with the prosecutor by confirming the testimony of hostile witnesses. While he rejects the defense arguments, he finds the prosecution interpretation interesting if false. The two interpretations are actually very close to one another, because both are designed to incorporate the facts within a socially meaningful structure. For both sides this entails a reading of Meursault's character, partly as a way of discovering the motive in this case, partly as a way of predicting his future conduct. From what we know of Meursault after part 1, we recognize the incongruity of these interpretations; but Meursault does not make use of the opportunities accorded to him during the trial to put forward his own version. Moreover, Meursault the narrator makes no effort to rectify the mistakes of Meursault the defendant; the case he presents to the reader is essentially the case his lawyer presented, but less, because of his lapses of attention and derogatory comments.

Magistrate. Framing the actual courtroom scene are two meetings with officials connected to the judicial system. The first is the examining magistrate. American courts have no exact equivalent to this officer, who is employed by the state but is not a prosecutor. His job is to investigate impartially and advise both sides. For him the pause between the first shot and the other four remains a mystery that Meursault cannot clear up; when repeatedly pressed to do so he maintains a stubborn silence. The magistrate then tries to elicit some expression of remorse from Meursault, with no greater success, and finally urges him to put his faith in Christ and repent. The magistrate interprets the murder in a religious rather than a social framework; he responds to

Meursault's account of the murder by saying, "Fine, fine," or "Good" (67; GS 83), no doubt accepting it as a manifestation of the sinful nature of humanity since the Fall. The portrait of this zealous Christian is rather comic; his excitement, his abrupt gestures, and his non sequiturs make him seem somewhat mad. Meursault's refusal to believe in God, or to claim to believe in God, leaves him in temporary confusion. Meursault refuses the obvious role of repentant sinner, but the magistrate's religious ideology still finds a place for him as the Antichrist. The reader may well regard the magistrate as a fool, but Meursault settles quite happily into this role. He protests less about being labeled a figure of supreme evil than about saying he loves Marie or regrets his crime.

Chaplain. The final interpreter who appears in the novel is the chaplain. He tries, somewhat like the magistrate at the beginning of part 2, to discover a religious meaning in Meursault's story. Meursault has, of course, been condemned at this point; his remorse would serve no further practical purpose on earth, but his repentance would, in the chaplain's view, win him forgiveness in the life hereafter. The chaplain accepts the judicial interpretation of the shooting as a premeditated murder and looks for a wider philosophical meaning. His repeated effort to get Meursault's assent provokes the most strenuous rejection of all; indeed, Meursault grows violent and must be restrained by the guards. In the chaplain's interpretation, Meursault's crime, like all life on earth, must be subordinated to the afterlife, where a final judgment will be rendered and eternal reward or punishment meted out. Of all the interpretations the chaplain's is thus the most absolute; it admits no possibility of error and there is no avenue of appeal. Meursault says that his rage was prompted by the fact that the chaplain seemed "so certain about everything" (120; GS 151). But the chaplain has in fact asked the right questions to challenge Meursault and draw him out of his apathetic silence, for his visit prompts the meditation on which the novel ends.

Defendant. Meursault himself is, of course, the logical person to provide a correct interpretation of his own actions. To the extent that we think we have a correct version, it is the one he gives us as narrator of the novel. In his trial, however, he seldom speaks. With his lawyer he has an urge to explain something, but "really there wasn't much point, and I gave up the idea out of laziness" (66; GS 81). With the examining magistrate, as we have seen, he refuses to answer the question about why he paused between the first and the second shots. Near the end of the trial, the judge offers Meursault the opportunity to speak for himself. Uncharacteristically, Meursault "did wish to speak," and said "almost at random, in fact, that I never intended to kill the Arab" (102; GS 129). The presiding judge then asks Meursault to "state precisely the motives" for his crime, admitting that "he hadn't quite grasped the nature" of the defense. Meursault repeats the explanation given in part 1: "I blurted out that it was because of the sun" but he realizes "how ridiculous I sounded" (103; GS 129–30). Here, as with the magistrate and his lawyer, Meursault understands what sort of explanation is required of him; yet he refuses to give it.

THE VERDICT

The guilty verdict is inevitable. The severity of the punishment is shocking, but Meursault does in fact pose a threat to society, in exactly the terms used by the magistrate: "Do you want my life to be meaningless?" (69; GS 86). Meursault's silences and nonsensical explanations keep him a stranger to the moral code under which he is judged. As he demonstrates in adapting to prison life, he is immune to punishment; by the time he understands that he is deprived of cigarettes as a punishment, he no longer craves them. The sense of life as disconnected moments, which let him feel that the murder just happened, also makes him feel that the imprisonment and the eventual execution just happen. He perceives no moral or symbolic links between events. He killed the Arab, he went to jail, he was condemned to death. In his mind these events have no more and no less relation to each other than this other sequence: he buried his mother, he slept with Marie, he did a favor for Raymond.

What makes sleeping with Marie incompatible with the mother's burial is a social code of propriety, which Meursault does not believe in and does not live by. What makes jail and a death sentence the logical sequel to the murder is a social code of justice, which Meursault also does not believe in, and lives by only because he is forced to. If he remains outside the social contract, however, it is not easy to distinguish between those who judge him and simple killers. Meursault understands his death on the guillotine no better than the Arab understood the senseless pistol shots, and without that recognition of a moral purpose, his death will be a cold-blooded murder in the name of the French people, who are all thereby implicated. Camus's thought on the question of violence is complex, and he sometimes argued radical positions that raise exceedingly difficult practical issues. The case against capital punishment is one of the least troublesome, because the state has so many other ways to uphold justice, maintain order, or simply impose its will. By comparison, the situation of people in wartime or the plight of the oppressed pose harsher dilemmas, which Camus addressed repeatedly, without ever finding a fully satisfactory solution.

The Stranger makes a weak case against the death penalty, because the fictional court bears such slight resemblance to a real one. It is almost taken for granted that executions serve neither justice nor necessity; they are symbolic rituals. Meursault, identified as a threat to society, is cast out of it; he becomes the scapegoat or sacrificial victim whose death restores order and preserves meaning. The fact that he cannot or will not understand his role only confirms his identity as a threatening monster. It is all the more important to immolate him because he exposes the violence on which the system of law and order is founded.

Society, in short, interprets the events so as to construct a Meursault independent of his noninvolvement. He becomes the bearer of social meanings, like an animal in a religious sacrifice. Furthermore, it should be obvious that we readers supply the ultimate interpretation, after the author and the characters have fallen silent. Meursault's lawyer makes the similarity between readers and judges explicit when he tells the jury that he has peered into Meursault's soul and can "read it like an open book" (104; GS 131). We, too, are implicated in the procedures of interpreting. This trial should make us aware of our own complicity in the deadly ritual. It is no answer, however, simply to spare Meursault; if Meursault lives, then the Arab must be the sacrificial victim. In the reality of preindependence Algeria, such an outcome would have been far more probable. But Camus was less interested in a social or political analysis than in the spiritual problems raised by the scapegoat.

To return to the conventional literary trials that we described in the beginning of this chapter, *The Stranger* works against most of the standard expectations. Passions do not run high. The prosecutor displays the greatest vehemence, but he seems bombastic and theatrical, not genuinely passionate. Meursault, whose life is at stake, loses interest. The contrast between appearance and reality is also minimal. Having read part 1, we know another version of Meursault's life and character; yet the trial never brings it out. In fact, what is perhaps most striking is the persuasive force of the various "appearances"— the explanatory inventions of the prosecutor and the defense lawyer, for example. In the usual trial scene, when the reality emerges it overwhelms appearance; in *The Stranger*, "reality" seems to disintegrate under the prosecutor's withering sarcasm and the defense attorney's incompetence.

Paradoxically, many readers respond to the trial as if the conviction of Meursault threatened individual freedom. Yet the crime of murder is unambiguously reprehensible; the case can hardly turn on Meursault's right to go about shooting people without cause. It should be evident that under almost any code of justice Meursault deserves to be condemned and punished, although not necessarily by death. Camus muddies the issue by raising questions about Meursault's behavior in other noncriminal circumstances. The reader's habit of identifying with the accused no doubt facilitates this narrative sleight of hand; the literary commonplace is that the prosecution misunderstands. The question is ultimately not about Meursault's freedom and sincerity in conflict with society's need for law and lies, however;

rather, it has to do with the integrity of character. Are the two incidents, the funeral and the murder, related or not? Does the moral attitude that prevails during the murder also prevail in Meursault's other actions? Or is Meursault correct in viewing each moment in his life as disconnected from the others?

It is difficult to say whether the prosecutor or Meursault simplifies more. The prosecutor insists that there is one Meursault, who is guilty; Meursault feels a different person each new moment, and cannot really connect the man in the cell to the one who pulled the trigger. Certainly the jury must render a clear verdict on a person whose character is elusive. If the court errs, however, it is in the penalty, not in the guilty verdict. It is right to hold Meursault responsible, and doing so accomplishes the final function of making the abstract concrete. Before his brush with the law, Meursault's moral irresponsibility flourishes, because it never becomes apparent. He seems like one of us, and yet he is a stranger. Indeed, from moment to moment he is a stranger to himself. Symbolically, the trial naturalizes Meursault. At the same time as it makes him a scapegoat and casts him out, it makes him one of the community. For the judgment rendered against him, confinement and ultimately death, turns out to be the universal sentence against humanity. Meursault is only made aware by the trial; he recognizes his human mortality and its implications. And so it is to a consideration of Meursault and his character that we must now turn.

7

MEURSAULT

HERO AND STRANGER

Even under close scrutiny, Meursault's account of the murder reveals very little that seems to explain the act or its causes. The trial, which is in fact an extended formal inquiry into the murder, resolves the matter in legal terms, but leaves the reader acutely aware of a disparity between the explanations advanced by the lawyers and Meursault's mentality. Meursault's character may then be the key to *The Stranger*'s meaning. Is he admirable, a hero of the absurd, a martyr to sincerity? Or is he the opposite, a model of insensitivity and errors to be avoided? Is he somewhere in between, a sort of case study? If so, a case of what—a hapless individual caught up in social forces he cannot comprehend, or an irresponsible egotist who wastes his chances for happiness? Is he an "everyman" figure, symbolic of human beings in the modern world, or is he an extreme case, whose fate tests the limits of our moral sensibility? Critics have proposed readings of *The Stranger* that rely on all these different analyses of the central character. This commentary will not try to settle the question, but to clarify the bases for discussion and to understand the function of Meursault's ambiguity.

Camus himself wrote a foreword for an American textbook

edition of *The Stranger,* in which he said that Meursault is "the only Christ we deserve," that he is condemned because he "does not play the game" and "refuses to lie," and that he is "a man who, without any heroic attitude, dies for the truth" (Pléiade, p. 1928). Camus admits in the foreword that he is making "paradoxical" statements, which is to say, contrary to common sense, bizarre, and deliberately provocative. Many early readers apparently shared his view, however; Meursault was regarded as a hero of a disenchanted era—the Great Depression, World War II, and the cold war. Sartre had already called Meursault a man who does not play the game, and the American editors echo Camus's foreword in their own introduction. But the novel has survived into a different moral atmosphere, and we need not continue reading *The Stranger* as if Meursault were a hero or a martyr. One significant rereading in the early 1960s recast Meursault as an exemplar of romantic egotism, who blames society and even God for his troubles, rather than admit his own guilt or responsibility. According to this interpretation, instead of a heroic truthteller, Meursault is a self-deluded liar, claiming to want privacy while desperately craving attention. Still more recent critics avoid discussing Meursault in such morally judgmental terms; he is taken as the exponent of a certain philosophical stance toward human existence. The mark of the novel's greatness is in part that the character can stand such reinterpretation. Meursault's story has the depth and complexity of human reality.

ORDINARY LIFE

Despite the title, Meursault does not appear a stranger or outsider to the other characters in the novel, at least until after the murder. He lives alone, but he has friends, especially Emmanuel and Céleste. He is a regular customer at Céleste's restaurant, where he pays by the month. Before he goes to Marengo, he lunches there, and "everybody felt very sorry for me" (3; GS 2); he decides not to eat there the following Sunday, since "they'd be sure to ask questions" (21; GS 25). But he returns for lunch on Monday, with Emmanuel, and he invites

Marie there for dinner a few days later, going alone when she declines. Céleste, of course, testifies on Meursault's behalf at the trial, ineffectually, since he can say only that Meursault was a friend. The portrait of Meursault through his relation with Céleste is, however, clearly that of an unexceptional but agreeable young man, somewhat more taciturn than most, perhaps, but far from isolated or antisocial.

Other aspects of his life support the same description. He holds a job, and has apparently worked there for some time. He seems to get along with his fellow workers; his friend Emmanuel works for the same company, and he had met Marie there some time previously. Moreover, despite Meursault's anxiety about asking for time off for the funeral and using the telephone for a private conversation, his boss gives no sign of disapproval and even offers him an opportunity for advancement, normally a sign of approval. Only when Meursault turns down the offer does the boss criticize his lack of ambition.

Meursault appears also to have good relations with women, at least by the standards of his social milieu. In prison he thinks "so much about a woman, about women, about all the ones I had known, about all the circumstances in which I had enjoyed them, that my cell would be filled with their faces and crowded with my desires" (77; GS 96). On the Sunday after the funeral, he watches the passers-by; two or three of the girls, whom he knows, look up and wave. Marie Cardona seems in all respects a normal young woman. Raymond and Masson find her attractive, and she gets along well with Masson's wife. She had met Meursault working as a typist in his office, and they had liked each other then, although "she'd left soon afterwards and we didn't have the time" (19; GS 23). Obviously, since she quickly agrees to go out with Meursault, sleeps with him, and wants to marry him, she likes him. Like the boss, she finds his diffidence disturbing, and calls him "peculiar" (42; GS 53) when he confesses that he would say yes to any girl who wanted to marry him. But she quickly overcomes her misgivings, and remains loyal to him throughout his year in prison and the trial, although she is allowed only one visit and he claims to have virtually forgotten her.

With the staff members at the Marengo home, Meursault also appears to have routine relations. During the trial, of course, they testify against him, and interpret his actions as callous indifference to his mother's death. At the funeral, however, they seem supportive and understanding. The director cuts off Meursault's excuses for placing his mother there: "the truth of the matter is, she was happier here" (4; GS 3). The caretaker is at first puzzled when he does not want to view his mother's body, but then says, "I understand" (6; GS 6), and engages Meursault in extensive conversation, shares a cigarette with him, and brings him coffee. The snatches of conversation and brief encounters he describes with the other patients, the nurse, and the undertaker's man, all have an air of absolute banality.

There are two other significant characters in part 1, Salamano and Raymond. They too regard Meursault as an ordinary person. Salamano seeks him out for consolation when his dog is lost, and he claims to have defended Meursault against neighborhood gossip when he put his mother in the home. Raymond pursues Meursault still more aggressively, asking his help writing a letter, wanting his approval, and inviting him to the beach. Although Salamano is ineffectual and Raymond makes a poor impression, both appear at the trial as friendly witnesses.

In short, if one were to describe Meursault on the basis of everything up to the murder, he would hardly merit the label *stranger* or *outsider*. True, he is a bit of a loner, not very talkative, and occasionally insensitive. One could equally well call him a strong silent type; his faults are rather typical of men, and are not carried to such extremes that Meursault could be deemed unusual. In the same way, one could perhaps call him lazy, but just as well easygoing or fun-loving. He is intelligent, likable, and reasonably conscientious; he is not gregarious, but not isolated either. If he had not killed a man, he could have passed his life unnoticed.

PLAYING THE GAME

The Boss. Meursault experiences his life as a series of essentially unconnected and therefore meaningless events. This is not to say that he does not appreciate the fact that others follow social rules and perceive meanings. In fact, Meursault shows a substantial willingness to "play the game" on a number of occasions. At the beginning of the novel, he detects annoyance in his boss about giving him two days off for the funeral. Or at least he imagines it, and says, "It's not my fault" (3; GS 1). Then he engages in a dialogue with himself about whose duty it was to express sympathy, and concludes that it was the boss's duty, not his own. The incident is minor, but placed conspicuously in the novel. Nothing results directly from it; later evidence suggests that the boss was not annoyed. It shows, however, the extent of Meursault's concern about social forms and his readiness to observe the etiquette.

On his return from Marengo Meursault realizes that the two days for the funeral take him into the weekend; thus he has four days away from his job, and he assumes that to be the source of the boss's vexation. Again, he is wrong; on Monday his employer inquires solicitously whether he is tired, and asks about his mother's age. Meursault gives an imprecise figure, "'about sixty,' so as not to make a mistake" (25; GS 30), once again showing his desire to maintain social decorum. Somewhat later, when Meursault declines the offer to move to the Paris office, the boss scolds him. Meursault stands firm, to be sure; it is a question of a major upheaval, not a mere courtesy. He says, however, "I would rather not have upset him" (52) and he feels the need to expound at some length the rationale for his decision. In other words, the evidence in Meursault's narrative suggests that he did not always accurately gauge his employer's opinion, but that he was consistently concerned about it and quite prepared to be accommodating.

Marie. The same is true with Marie, although Meursault makes less effort to respect her feelings. "Playing the game" with a more powerful opponent, his boss, he is cautious; with a weaker partner, his girlfriend, he is bold. He distresses Marie by denying that he loves her, and he puzzles her by agreeing to marry her anyway. He tells her that love has no meaning to him, and that marriage is not serious. On both occasions, he understands what she wants him to say. After discussing marriage, they go for a walk. According to Meursault, "the women were beautiful and I asked Marie if she'd noticed. She said yes and that she understood what I meant" (42; GS 54). The implication appears to be that Meursault is still clinging to his bachelor freedom, and warning Marie that he will not be faithful to her. Whatever one may think of his attitude, he certainly knows what the usual expectations are. One could argue that his scruples about the implications of words like love and rites like marriage signify exactly the opposite of meaninglessness; Meursault almost alone in his society insists that the meanings be respected, that the definitions be precise, and that the reality fit the definition. At the end of their betrothal scene Marie turns down an invitation to dinner; Meursault, who wonders where she is going instead of joining him, does not think of asking, and she reproaches him for it. Here, Meursault feels and looks embarrassed. In this small battle of the sexes, he has slipped up and been caught. He won the point about the beautiful women; she wins this one. His silence itself is part of a male game of dominance: he knows it, she knows it, and she forgives him because his embarrassment is a concession. Camus's published opinion notwithstanding, Meursault does indeed play games with Marie.

Marengo. At the Marengo home Meursault is frequently concerned about whether he is obeying the unwritten rules. In this case the trial will prove that he has violated the code. In his talk with the director Meursault feels accused, but the director reassures him. In the room with the coffin Meursault declines to view the body, provoking a stare from the caretaker; "I was embarrassed because I felt I shouldn't have said that" (6; GS 6), he relates. He and the caretaker enter into a discussion of funerals, which the caretaker's wife interrupts as unseemly; Meursault reassures him. Not long afterward they have coffee and Meursault wants a cigarette, "But I hesitated because I didn't know if I could do it with Maman right there. I thought about it; it didn't matter" (8; GS 9). He is wrong, because at the trial his smoking is held against him; even so, his account shows that he worries about it and to that extent understands the possible implications of the gesture. During the vigil, a woman begins to sob; Meursault says, "I wished I didn't have to listen to her anymore. But I didn't dare say anything" (10; GS 11). In the morning the old people pass by to shake Meursault's hand; he is surprised, but goes along with the gesture, while interpreting it as the expression of an intimacy that he himself does not feel.

Were it not that Meursault tells all these details, and that the prosecutor builds his case on them, it would be ridiculous to focus so much attention on them. On the basic question the prosecutor is actually correct: Meursault did not feel grief at his mother's death, and he never claims that he did. The methods of judicial proof trivialize that question into a series of pointless details: Did he weep? Did he sleep? Did he smoke? Did he view the body? Did he linger at the grave? Did he know his mother's age? If the prosecutor had simply addressed the question to Meursault, as Meursault's own lawyer does, he would not have appeared so petty-minded and would have obtained a self-damning reply: "I probably did love Maman, but that didn't mean anything. At one time or another all normal people have wished their loved ones were dead. . . . The day I buried Maman, I was very tired and sleepy, so much so that I wasn't really aware of what was going on. What I can say for certain is that I would rather Maman hadn't died" (65; GS 80).

Meursault's lawyer, appalled, asks "if he could say that that day I had held back my natural feelings. I said, 'No, because it's not true'" (65; GS 80). The diehard commitment to truth that Meursault professes here is by no means consistent. Indeed, it seems to have been provoked by his feeling, probably quite justified, that "none of this had anything to do with my case" (65; GS 81). At the funeral itself Meursault makes a considerable effort to conduct himself in an appropriate fashion. For that matter his being there at all can be explained only by a sense of obligation to show filial respect.

Salamano. Meursault's readiness to follow the ordinary dictates of social courtesy is best seen in his relations with Salamano, the elderly neighbor who resembles his mangy dog. Salamano seems pathetic and somewhat repulsive. In his first appearance he is cursing and beating the dog in the apartment stairway. Meursault does no more than utter a greeting and make a friendly inquiry, to which he obtains a rather rude reply. A few days later the dog runs away. Unexpectedly, Salamano is distraught, and Meursault does his best to advise him how to recover it. The dog is not at the pound, however, and Salamano returns to Meursault for consolation. Meursault invites him in, listens to his story, asks some questions to keep the conversation going despite feeling bored, and even pleases the old man by saying the dog "was well bred" (45; GS 57). Although Meursault does not trouble to agree when Salamano suggests that he must be feeling very sad since his mother's death, he urges Salamano to stay on a bit longer and says he is sorry about the dog. Meursault's kindness toward Salamano contrasts with his usual indifference and reserve, and furthermore reveals a fine sense of tact. Nobody, surely, would criticize Meursault for the polite lies he tells the bereaved Salamano.

Raymond. Another resident of the building, Raymond Sintès, is still more an outcast in the neighborhood, since he is reputed to be a pimp. It is he who involves Meursault in the quarrel with the Arab, whom Meursault eventually murders. Raymond is far more presumptuous than anyone else in the story. He appears for the first time right after the first encounter with Salamano, and invites Meursault to share his dinner. He soon confesses that he wants Meursault's advice, which turns out to be a significant service. As he starts to explain the situation, "he asked me again if I wanted to be pals" (29; GS 36). Meursault replies that "it was fine with me," more or less as he does to Marie's marriage proposal. As Raymond tells the lengthy tale of his keeping a Moorish mistress, her infidelity, his beating her, and his fight with her brother, he asks several times for Meursault's approval:

> "He was asking for it."
> It was true and I agreed. (29; GS 36)

> He wanted to know what I thought of the whole thing. I said I didn't think anything but that it was interesting. He asked if I

thought she was cheating on him, and it seemed to me she was; if I
thought she should be punished and what I would do in his place,
and I said you can't ever be sure, but I understood his wanting to
punish her. (32; GS 40)

Perhaps Meursault is simply making himself agreeable; if so, he
is telling social lies that are a good deal less tolerable than saying he
loves Marie or mourns his mother. Or perhaps he sincerely shares the
ethical code that Raymond propounds; if so, his professed inability to
discern meaning in human relationships is highly specific, if not simply
hypocritical. His role grows still more indefensible as Raymond passes
from talk to action by asking Meursault to write a letter: "He asked
if I'd mind doing it right then and I said no. . . . I tried my best to
please Raymond because I didn't have any reason not to please him"
(32; GS 41). Raymond immediately begins addressing Meursault in
familiar terms, claps him on the shoulder, and says, "Now you're a
pal." Meursault keeps silent at first, but Raymond persists: "I didn't
mind being his pal, and he seemed set on it" (33; GS 41). To Marie he
would most likely have said that being pals really had no meaning,
and that he supposed not, but this is between men. As the scene begins,
Raymond tells Meursault "he wanted to ask my advice about the
whole business, because I was a man, I knew about things" (29; GS
36); and as he leaves, he remarks that "men always understand each
other" (33; GS 42).

Raymond continues to impose on Meursault's goodwill. Meursault's letter has the desired effect: the woman comes to Raymond's
apartment and he beats her up. A policeman is summoned and puts
the cocky Raymond in his place with a vigorous slap in the face; Raymond soon appeals to Meursault for reassurance that he has not lost
his reputation as a tough guy. But he also wants another favor: "He
told me that I'd have to act as a witness for him. It didn't matter to
me, but I didn't know what I was supposed to say. According to Raymond, all I had to do was to state that the girl had cheated on him. I
agreed to act as a witness for him" (37; GS 40). Where Raymond is
concerned, Meursault is certainly no martyr to the truth, and however

reluctantly he undertakes the role of "pal," he seems quite prepared to meet all its social obligations.

DESIRES

We must recognize that our knowledge of Meursault's place in society is mediated by the fact that he tells his own story. All we know of Marie's or the boss's reactions is what Meursault notices, or believes he notices, and remembers, or chooses to relate. Complicated processes of unconscious bias or deliberate falsification could enter into the narration. What Meursault says directly about himself may be equally distorted in some ways, but it must at least present Meursault as he himself intends. The framework of the novel, which resembles a diary at the beginning, and later seems a silent meditation addressed to no one, tends to convey sincerity. The absence of an obvious audience leads us to suppose that the speaker is trying to discover the truth for himself. Whom could he be trying to deceive, and to what purpose? In Meursault's case, his credibility is enhanced by the number of times he tells a truth that brings him harm. Why would he tell the magistrate he felt no remorse and then lie to himself?

Meursault, as we have seen, is aware of feelings and opinions in others, but he acknowledges few emotions in himself. Particularly in situations where one expects feelings, he professes to have none. Thus he feels little sorrow at his mother's death, little joy at Marie's love, little pleasure at the boss's offer of a promotion, little remorse for his crime. He expresses no anger and hardly any regret even at the loss of his freedom. He seems to feel no resentment toward Raymond, who drew him into the quarrel with the Arabs, nor toward his lawyer, who handles his case poorly, nor toward the court, which condemns him. His most consistent feelings are fatigue and boredom. Only the chaplain provokes him to a passionate outburst.

By contrast, he acknowledges many sensual appetites and demonstrates their existence indirectly by talking about their objects. He likes to eat, to drink, to make love, to swim, to lie in the sun, and especially to sleep. He notices and recalls sights, sounds, smells, and tactile sensations. His preference for a dry hand towel once prompted him to request it from his boss. In prison he waxes lyrical about "the smell and color of the summer evening . . . all the familiar sounds of a town I loved" (97; GS 122), and he is distracted at the climax of his trial by "by an ice cream vendor blowing his tin trumpet out in the street," which evokes a rush of memories of "the simplest and most lasting joys: the smells of summer, the part of town I loved, a certain evening sky, Marie's dresses and the way she laughed" (104; GS 132). The memories of lost pleasures come to him only fitfully, however, prompted by chance sounds outside the window, like the ice-cream truck's horn. Even his sensual appetites seem to be born of the moment, to be stimulated by accidental opportunities, not to arise from persistent desire. He claims not to miss Marie very much, and tells the chaplain that he has been unable to see her face in his cell wall.

Meursault has a small list of dislikes, too. Sundays bore him. Just as he enjoys a dry towel, he complains of a wet one. He often avoids talking, with the soldier on the bus to Marengo, the friendly but inquisitive crowd at Celeste's, the tearful women at the beach, the examining magistrate. He reserves his strongest aversion for policemen, offering it to Marie as a reason not to summon help when Raymond beats the Moorish woman. Confronted with any unpleasant prospect, Meursault usually tries to withdraw, into silence, into his room, into sleep. He regards his apartment as too large once his mother has moved out; he confines himself to one room. It is partly for this reason that he adapts so readily to prison life; his cell is like a refuge where he can savor in solitude the sensations left to him. Toward the end of his trial he says, "All I wanted was to get it over with and get back to my cell and sleep" (105; GS 132).

Meursault has no passions. He has no long-range goal and no obsessive longings. None of the plans that most people make seem meaningful to him; he has no ambition, no wish for power, status, fame, or wealth, no need to be loved or to found a family. He has no curiosity, no wish to travel, no interest in changing his life. The question never comes up whether he might have ideals, such as political commitment or patriotic zeal; obviously not. He does not even seem to share his neighborhood's loyalty to its soccer team. And, of course, he has no religious faith. One of the very rare clues about Meursault's past suggests that this relentless indifference arose from disappointment. When he turns down the job in Paris, he says, "When I was a student, I had lots of ambitions like that. But when I had to give up my studies I learned very quickly that none of it really mattered" (41; GS 52). We never learn what caused him to drop his studies, but it seems likely that he has retreated into a sort of protective insensitivity as a result of that frustration.

IN PRISON

Prison changes Meursault remarkably little. He talks several times about his difficulty in learning to think prisoner's thoughts, but he brings a certain aptitude or predisposition to the task. He relinquishes his sensual pleasures without much struggle. Sex and cigarettes prove to be the sternest tests, but he finds masturbation a suitable substitute for women and deprivation eventually kills his longing for tobacco. He feels about himself that "if I had had to live in the trunk of a dead tree, with nothing to do but look up at the sky flowering overhead, little by little I would have gotten used to it" (77; GS 95). Living as he does outside the symbolic orders of meaning, he is essentially unpunishable. Everything is simply a condition of existence; nothing is retribution or reward. He continues to pursue the pleasures left to him, meals, the daily walk in the courtyard, and especially sleep: "I've been sleeping sixteen to eighteen hours a day" (79; GS 99). Initially, his refusal to talk to the chaplain appears no different from the many times before, both in and out of prison, when he lapsed into silence.

He also remains aware of social expectations in the same way as before. With his lawyer Meursault realizes that he makes a bad impression: "I wished I could have made him stay, to explain that I wanted things between us to be good" (65–66; GS 81). Soon afterward he is interviewed by the magistrate. It is obvious that he disturbs this official, who tries to extract a profession of faith from him. In this conversation, however, Meursault confesses shamelessly to a common type of social hypocrisy: "As always, whenever I want to get rid of someone I'm not really listening to, I made it appear as if I agreed" (69; GS 86). With both these men Meursault eventually develops a cordial relationship, sitting in on their discussions of his case over a year's time; he confides that "I was almost surprised that I had ever enjoyed anything other than those rare moments when the judge would lead me to the door of the office, slap me on the shoulder, and say to me cordially, 'That's all for today, Monsieur Antichrist'" (71; GS 88). Meursault's pleasures are decidedly simple ones, but he still craves approval from those he perceives as superior.

With others he is more brusque. On the day of his arrest he is put in a room "where there were already several other prisoners, most of them Arabs. They laughed when they saw me. Then they asked me what I was in for. I said I'd killed an Arab and they were all silent" (72; GS 89). Meursault does not shrink from saying more than he has to or from speaking with aggressive bluntness on some occasions; he could have said he had killed "someone," or killed "a man," or "committed murder," or he could have affected the stony silence he adopts with the magistrate and his lawyer when he finds their questions awkward. In this situation his latent racism and class consciousness free his tongue. He plainly knows the implications of his remark. That evening the other prisoners have to show him how to make a bed from his mat; revealing that fact is as close as he ever comes to expressing gratitude, regret, or solidarity with these fellow prisoners.

On the one visit Marie is allowed, Meursault has little to say to her; he is distracted by the noise and confusion around him, and focuses mainly on the sensual desires she arouses—"I wanted to squeeze her shoulders through her dress. I wanted to feel the thin material and I didn't really know what else I had to hope for other than that" (75; GS 92). Wanting to prolong her stay, he forces himself to utter a few responses, "mainly just to say something" (75; GS 93). In the courtroom he pays attention to the attitudes, real or imagined, that the jurors, the press corps, the witnesses, and the prosecutor hold toward him. A harsh look from the prosecutor makes him realize for the first time "how much all these people hated me" (90; GS 112). By confirming that he had offered the cigarette himself, Meursault wins the gratitude of the caretaker. He interprets a gaze from Céleste as "asking me what else he could do," and feels for the first time in his life that he "wanted to kiss a man"—but of course he "said nothing" and "made no gesture of any kind" (93; GS 116) to expose an impulse he considers so unmasculine. Near the end of the trial Meursault finally speaks on his own behalf, saying that he shot the Arab because of the sun, while "realizing how ridiculous I sounded" (103; GS 130). After his lawyer's final speech, other lawyers compliment him and one calls Meursault to witness; "I agreed, but my congratulations weren't sincere" (105; GS 133). He detects a reproachful anxiety on Marie's face, understandable since he has avoided her eye throughout the trial, and he cannot even muster a smile when he finally looks at her. After the death sentence is announced, he believes he can interpret the expressions on the faces around him as "a look of consideration" (107; GS 135).

What these details show is that Meursault, in prison and on trial, remains aware of other people's reactions to him, and reacts himself. It makes no difference whether his perceptions are accurate or not; we have no way of testing most of them, but nothing happens to disprove them. Moreover, they seem generally plausible, which is to say that he understands moral and social codes much as most people do. He responds somewhat differently, perhaps, but those responses seem to reflect an unconscious code, that of the working-class European male in preindependence Algeria, more than a systematic refusal to lie or a thoroughgoing incomprehension of what others expect.

Meursault is a very ordinary person trying to find a limited happiness in an indifferent world. His attitude should inspire no admiration, and certainly is not to be imitated. He is a sort of antihero. Where typical heroes devote their lives to a cause, Meursault has no faith in any cause, and indeed recognizes no meaning. He wants to live for the present moment, but Camus presents him without enough philosophical sophistication to rationalize his attitude. What makes him strange is in fact his blindness to his own beliefs. Most of the time implicitly, but sometimes explicitly, he regards his own impulses as "natural." When Marie asks whether he would say yes to any girl who proposed marriage to him, he replies, "Naturally" (42, my translation of "naturellement"; GS 53). When he comes upon the Arab on the beach, he says, "Naturally, I gripped Raymond's gun" (58; GS 74). His dislike of the police, his lack of ambition, his sensuality, his tendency to keep silent, his attitudes toward women and Arabs, his treatment of his mother, his friendship with Raymond—all these may well be justifiable, but Meursault regards them as givens. He is, in short, intellectually lazy and irresponsible, as he admits at least once when he decides not to try to explain himself to his lawyer: "I gave up the idea out of laziness" (66; GS 81).

LAZINESS

This laziness so pervades Meursault's attitude that he assumes everything is equal if he has no feeling about it. One woman is as good a wife as another, one man makes as good a friend as another, one job is like another, to go back to the beach or not comes to the same thing, even to shoot or not to shoot. Meursault is completely prey to his own conditioned responses, utterly unaware that they, too, express the very sort of meaning and purpose that he does not want to acknowledge. This apathetic ignorance produces a small monster of pure egotism. With enough power at his disposal, he might be a tyrant, like Caligula.

The Meursault of part 1 is no hero and no victim. He would hardly be worth knowing about except that he kills a man. Had he not committed this crime, he could have lived his life more or less as he wanted, or at least as he had been living up until then. Ordinary people do not commit murder, especially with so little provocation and so little purpose. It is one thing to lose one's belief in God, in the work ethic, in family values, in love; to lose one's belief in the right of others to live is something quite different, a pathological condition that threatens everyone, at least if one acts accordingly. In societies like the one Camus describes in *The Stranger,* nonbelievers are left in peace so long as they grant others the same right. It is true that many societies are organized on the principle that only religious faith or something similar restrains a human propensity for violence and anarchy. The prosecutor in *The Stranger* argues that way; but his logic would not be persuasive if Meursault had not in fact already killed someone.

The Meursault of part 1 is not even much of a stranger or outsider. He does not share a good many conventional beliefs, but his unbelief seems to be shared by enough people to form a circle of companions. The claim that Meursault is a radical innocent who does not comprehend and therefore does not play the game, a claim made by Camus himself and by critics as astute as Sartre, does not seem to stand up under examination. In part 2, Meursault becomes an outsider to society, when he is on trial for murder. The narrative makes it seem that he is condemned for not playing the game, but again, that argument does not stand up. A more convincing view of Meursault as a stranger is that he becomes a stranger to himself in part 2. The image that is thrown back to him as he hears his life narrated by others, like the one he sees reflected in his prisoner's tin plate, seems foreign to him. This alienation of the self was, of course, a common theme in the literature of the era, as in Sartre's famous line "Hell is Others." It probably explains the readiness of many readers to identify with Meursault.

THE UNREPENTANT MURDERER

For one would normally hesitate to feel much sympathy for an unmotivated and unrepentant murderer. Why did Camus invent such a character? One reason for Camus's interest is that gratuitous murder was a literary theme, treated in such works as Gide's satirical novel *Lafcadio's Adventures* (*Les Caves du Vatican,* 1914) and Sartre's story "Erostratus," published in the collection entitled *The Wall* (*Le Mur,* 1939). That is to say that writers were interested in the ethical problems from an abstract philosophical perspective, in a tradition descended from Nietzsche and including notably the surrealists. The reader is not expected to form a sympathetic emotional identification with these murderous characters, but rather to observe the working out of a moral experiment. In the next chapter we will consider some conclusions that might be drawn from Camus's version.

Throughout his career Camus was deeply interested by the problem of taking human life. His first attempt at a novel, *A Happy Death*, contained a murder. His plays—*Caligula, The Just Assassins, The Misunderstanding*—deal with murders. In *Exile and the Kingdom*, a collection of short stories, the central figure in "The Renegade" and the Arab in "The Guest" are murderers. The subject is discussed in *The Plague* and in *The Fall*. By and large these crimes are not unmotivated, but with one exception the murderers seem unrepentant. The exception is the mother in *The Misunderstanding*, an innkeeper who, aided by her daughter, murders her guests and robs them. In the play on one occasion she commits the crime, only to discover that the victim is her long-lost son. An obvious implication is that anonymous strangers are our kinfolk in disguise. Meursault reads the story of *The Misunderstanding* on a scrap of newspaper he finds in his jail cell:

> A man had left a Czech village to seek his fortune. Twenty-five years later, and now rich, he had returned with a wife and a child. His mother was running a hotel with his sister in the village where he'd been born. In order to surprise them, he had left his wife and child at another hotel and gone to see his mother, who didn't recognize him when he walked in. As a joke he'd had the idea of taking a room. He had shown off his money. During the night his mother and his sister had beaten him to death with a hammer in order to rob him and had thrown his body in the river. The next morning the wife had come to the hotel and, without knowing it, gave away the traveler's identity. The mother hanged herself. The sister threw herself down a well. (79–80; GS 99–100)

Oddly, Meursault blames the murder victim: "I thought the traveler pretty much deserved what he got and that you should never play games" (80; GS 100). The mother and daughter of the clipping commit suicide, presumably in despair; Meursault exonerates them. He is, as it were, unrepentant for them—as the sister is in the play, where she echoes some of Meursault's lines, such as, "Words like love and joy and grief are meaningless to me" (128). Camus was always more concerned with the ways in which the murderer assumed responsibility for the crime, than in the self-evident moral prohibition against it. Meursault discovers his ultimate truth, not in regret, but in an affirmation of what he has done.

In the final chapter of *The Stranger* Meursault undergoes an inner change of some kind, experiencing a revelation through which all that has gone before takes on a new meaning. If this final state of mind represents an end to his exile or alienation, the novel can also be thought of as a journey or a quest. In the first pages Meursault does in fact set out on a journey, to Marengo. On the bus he falls asleep, and in his sleep slumps against a soldier. When he awakes, the soldier grins at him and asks if he had "been traveling long. I said, 'Yes,' just so I wouldn't have to say anything else" (4; GS 2). There are several familiar themes here: sleep, silence, the polite lie. Like many apparently innocuous lines in the novel, it tells a deeper truth than Meursault realizes, or than is at first apparent to the reader. Camus uses a similar scene to begin the first story of *Exile and the Kingdom*, "The Adulterous Woman," in which the main characters, Janine and Marcel, could well be Marie and Meursault, married and grown middle-aged. There, the bus trip unmistakably stands for a spiritual progress, and the routine incidents provoke a complex self-examination.

In Meursault's thoughts the murder occupies no place at all. So far as one can tell, he never feels any remorse, and he never dwells on what he terms the "annoyance" it has caused him. His fantasies of cheating death do not include erasing that crime from his past. Instead, he states in the closing lines of the novel that he finally understands his mother's feelings in her last days. Like Martha, the sister in *The Misunderstanding,* Meursault has less concern for the anonymous murder victim than for the lost mother. In order to understand Meursault's conclusion, we must first see how he has reconstructed his past.

8
RECONSTRUCTING THE PAST

THE MOMENT OF NARRATION

In the first chapter of part 2 the magistrate begins his interview by saying that Meursault had the reputation of being "a taciturn and withdrawn person"—a reputation that, as we have seen, is well deserved—to which Meursault replies, "It's just that I don't have much to say" (66; GS 82). In fact, Meursault's silences are selective and explicable in social terms, but the general characterization is nonetheless valid, and nowhere have we seen any evidence that Meursault talked much about himself. Indeed, he resists conceptualizing and articulating his own feelings and ideas, evading the mental effort required by assuming his desires to be natural and everything else to be unimportant. The whole novel is therefore founded on a strange inconsistency in Meursault: this taciturn self-centered person for some reason talks or writes at great length to explain his actions to someone else. The story he tells is in part a story of being forced to speak.

Evidence in the Text. First-person narration is a common enough method in fiction, but Camus has made it very hard to characterize exactly how and when Meursault speaks. The opening line of the novel appears to be from a person speaking in the present, or writing in a diary: "Maman died today" (3; GS 1). He goes on to discuss his plans to attend the funeral as a future event: "I'll take the two o'clock bus and get there in the afternoon. That way I can be there for the vigil and come back tomorrow night" (3; GS 1). The time when those words were uttered must have been between early morning, when the telegram arrived announcing the mother's death, and two o'clock, when the bus leaves.

The third paragraph comes after a certain lapse of time; it begins: "I caught the two o'clock bus" (3; GS 2). From this point to the end of the chapter, Meursault tells the events in the past tense, as in an ordinary narration. Once or twice he reveals a certain distance between the events he is describing and his memory of them. For example, he says of his mother's friends who watch over the coffin with him, "I even had the impression that the dead woman lying in front of them didn't mean anything to them. But I think now that that was a false impression" (11; GS 12–13); obviously there is a difference between his impression at the time it happened and his opinion at the time he tells about it. A few lines later he says, "I remember opening my eyes at one point" (11; GS 13). At the end of the chapter he repeats comments about his memories: "I don't remember any of it anymore. Except for one thing" (18; GS 21) and "Several other images from that day have stuck in my mind" (18–19; GS 21). The chapter ends with his memory of the joy of going to bed at last.

The account of the funeral could have been recorded at any time after it happened. In theory Meursault could have written each little section soon after it occurred, adding it to what was already done, as the third paragraph is simply added to the second. But nothing in the story supports that theory; after the third paragraph Meursault stops using time adverbs like "today" and verbs in the future tense. On the contrary, as we have seen, he exposes the lapse of time between the action and the narration. In theory, again, it could be a very brief lapse; but the loss of detailed memories and the change in opinion suggest a longer period.

Yet chapter 2 begins again in the present: "Today is Saturday" (19; GS 22), and as in chapter 1, the opening paragraphs continue as if spoken directly to someone present or recorded in a diary: "It isn't my fault if they buried Maman yesterday instead of today" (19; GS 22) and "I had a hard time getting up, because I was tired from yesterday" (19, my translation; GS 23). This chapter goes on to relate Meursault's meeting Marie at the pool, their night together, and his Sunday watching the street, as mere past events. There are no clear signs of distance between the past time of the action and the present time of the narration, as there were in chapter 1, but there are also no more present-time adverbs or future-tense verbs.

Chapter 3 also begins with an adverb indicating present time: "I worked hard at the office today" (25; GS 30). The actions are all recounted in the past—lunch at Céleste's, a meeting on the stairs with Salamano and his dog, dinner with Raymond Sintès. But both Salamano and Sintès are described in the present: "Twice a day, at eleven and six, the old man takes the dog out for a walk. They haven't changed their route in eight years. You can see them in the rue de Lyon . . ." (27; GS 33); "[My other neighbor] often talks to me and sometimes stops by my place for a minute, because I listen to him. I find what he has to say interesting. Besides, I don't have any reason not to talk to him. His name is Raymond Sintès" (28; GS 34). Chapter 4 is almost entirely told in the past; only once does Meursault say, "Yesterday was Saturday" (34; GS 42), implying that "Today is Sunday." But virtually the entire chapter tells of past events—Meursault's second night with Marie, Raymond's abuse of the Moorish woman, his subsequent visit to Meursault, and Salamano's loss of his dog—and chapters 5 and 6 continue this mode of narration. No adverbs point to the present, and nothing indicates an unknown future. There is also no sign of the narrator's present, until the end of chapter 6 when he says, "And there, in that noise, sharp and deafening at the same time, is where it all started" (59; GS 76), implying that he is already aware of most of the consequences of the shooting.

We must conclude from this rather tedious inspection of adverbs and verb forms that the narrative perspective is inconsistent. Despite many indications of present-time narration, the dominant form is retrospective. The narrator hints once or twice that some time has passed, but never explicitly clarifies the time or the situation from which he is speaking. The passages told in the present seem to represent efforts to relive or reconstruct the past. For brief periods Meursault can think and therefore tell his past as if it were still present, but he quickly falls back into a more common narrative pattern, in which he relates each event in sequence, in the past. In doing so, he refrains nevertheless very systematically from using his retrospective knowledge to comment. "It all started" could have been said of the invitation to go to the beach, or of Raymond's request for Meursault to write the letter, or of other incidents in part 1. Since Salamano loses his dog in chapter 4, Meursault could have described their relationship differently in chapter 3.

Ambiguity. Camus surely wanted a certain ambiguity to hover over his narrator. It is important that the events of part 1 seem to occur naturally. They must not seem part of a plot or a destiny. They have to happen in the sort of random and disconnected way that most real things happen, or seem to happen, and that Meursault finds meaningless. At the same time, they have to be presented from Meursault's perspective; it is his sense of a meaning or a destiny that is at stake. Camus therefore devised a deceptive technique, in which Meursault's remembering and reliving is delivered directly to the reader without any explanatory frame.

The first few chapters begin with adverbs of time like "today" and verbs in the present or future tense, which create a strong impression of a narration that is simultaneous with the events, or following close afterward. The use of the nonliterary compound past tense powerfully enhances the impression; normally, in a narration such as this, the simple past would predominate, with the compound past used only for events linked to the present—for example, in the first sentence of chapter 2 in part 2, "There are some things I've never liked talking about" (72; GS 89). "I've never liked" would be a compound tense, the present perfect, in any style of narration, because the feeling presumably persists from the past to the present. In part 2 the signs of a significant lapse of time between action and narration become clearer and more frequent. At the end of chapter 1 in part 2, Meursault says, "at the end of the eleven months that this investigation lasted" (71; GS 88), putting at least that much time between his first interrogation and his writing the account of it. The chapters that follow begin in an obvious retrospective mode.

Meursault never says outright: "And then I wrote this account of my life." Some readers locate the composition of part 1 within those eleven months, arguing that it represents a sort of composite transcript of Meursault's repetitions of his story to the magistrate: "He pressed me to go back over that day. I went back over what I had already told him: Raymond, the beach, the swim, the quarrel, then back to the beach, the little spring, the sun, and the five shots from the revolver" (67; GS 82–83). That is to say, in telling his story from the funeral to the murder, Meursault does not yet know how the jury will decide. Certainly throughout part 1 he suppresses any evidence of foreknowledge of his impending conviction. But he adopts that pose from the very start, in matters both large and small, suppressing foreknowledge of events within part 1 as well as those in part 2, concealing advance knowledge of the murder and the arrest as well as of the eventual death sentence, concealing any awareness that helping Raymond would lead to trouble or that meeting Marie would lead to an engagement, concealing even the fact that Salamano's dog would run away. Thus part 1 cannot be taken as a realistic discourse produced at a time and in a manner explained within the story. It imitates a day-by-day account, but with lapses that prove it is not an actual diary or on-the-spot narrative. Whenever and however it was first produced, in its present form it is a retrospective account, internally inconsistent, with no clear indication of the narrator's present situation.

To most readers, therefore, it seems simpler and more satisfactory to assume that Meursault has been thinking the entire story, or telling it to himself in his cell after the chaplain's visit. That final chapter resumes the apparently present-tense narration. It begins: "For the third time I've refused to see the chaplain. I don't have anything to say to him; I don't feel like talking, and I'll be seeing him soon enough as it is. All I care about right now is escaping the machinery of justice" (108; GS 135–36). Those few lines contain present-tense and future-tense verbs and the adverb "now" just like the opening chapters. Meursault soon modulates into a past tense, but in a logical way: it is to explain why he has refused to see the chaplain, to tell what he has been thinking about recently. Then, at the end of a long description of his reasoning process, he says, "It was at one such moment that I once again refused to see the chaplain" (115; GS 144), as if the intervening passages had been thought or written since the chaplain's request for an interview, as if the time of thinking or writing were the time elapsed from event to telling. Then, suddenly, he says, "the chaplain came in" (115; GS 144), and the narrative continues in the past tense, relating the chaplain's visit, Meursault's angry outburst, and his eventual calm. It is told retrospectively, looking back over past events, but there is no way to tell how much time has passed between the chaplain's visit and Meursault's telling about it.

The final chapter repeats the typical narrative structure of the chapters in part 1, with their powerful impression of immediacy. On analysis, however, it is clear that in both places the narrator has used a device to make past experiences seem present, to force the reader to experience them with the anxiety and uncertainty of a lived moment, rather than with the comfort and security of hindsight. The structure of the narrative, in other words, seems to tie part 1 to the concluding chapter. Furthermore, the chaplain's visit provokes in Meursault an unaccustomed degree of passion and unleashes a spectacular barrage of words. Of all the moments narrated in the novel, it seems the one most fitting for Meursault's breakthrough into self-awareness and self-expression. It is here that he realizes his deepest feelings, and it is also here that for the first time he desires to make them known. It seems most suitable, therefore, to assume that the entire novel is a unified reconstruction of the past, told from the start with the consciousness of the insights Meursault gains at the very end. It partially realizes his feeling, expressed in the last paragraph, "And I felt ready to live it all again too" (122; GS 154).

Meursault relives only a small portion of his life, however, the part that began with his mother's death. Of his infancy, childhood, and youth we can infer very little. We know that, for unspecified reasons, he had to give up his studies. He tells Marie that he had once lived in Paris. For at least eight years he lived in the same apartment, the first five sharing it with his mother, who seldom spoke and who went to the Marengo home for the last three years. In the prison he remembers a few things his mother used to say, including the story of his father's witnessing an execution. In the early days of his imprisonment he thought about all the women he had known, but these memories remain hazy, even of Marie, the only woman he names.

THE FUNERAL

One might argue that Meursault focuses on his mother's funeral for the simple reason that the prosecutor turned it into an incriminating incident. There is no way to refute this argument, but Meursault does not orient his account by what was said in the courtroom. In retelling the incident, he neither confirms nor rebuts the prosecutor's argument. He presents his memory of what happened as plainly as possible, leaving it to the reader to judge whether his conduct was innocent or not. If this were a real prisoner's narrative, his own view of the events would inevitably have been altered by the trial and its aftermath. If Camus's goal had been to render reality as faithfully as possible, he would have had to incorporate that bias into the rhetoric of the narrative and made the psychology of the narrator a central problem of the novel; the narrator's reliability would have to be assessed at each moment. We have seen, however, that Camus does not appear to have been much concerned with that sort of realistic representation. By making Meursault's style so neutral in tone, and by allowing him to relate his version first, Camus created a strong presumption that Meursault tells the truth to the extent that he can. More than that, Camus exploited the conventions of the novel so that Meursault can remember more precisely and retell more coherently than would be plausible for a real person with Meursault's characteristics. In other words, we will accept the paradoxical notion that Meursault is moved to tell his story by the final revelation he has, and that the form he adopts is influenced by his frame of mind at the end, but that the substance of his recollections is not altered in any significant way.

Camus's method is much like the convention of perfect memory that was popular in the eighteenth century; Abbé Prévost's classic novel *Manon Lescaut* is an example with which Camus was surely familiar. The entire two-hundred-page novel is purportedly the verbatim transcription of an oral narrative, spoken by the hero Des Grieux, written down by a friend. Moreover, although Des Grieux is telling his own life story, and obviously knows how it has turned out up to the moment of narration, he tells it without giving away the eventual outcome of each episode. He is less systematic than Meursault; his situation at the end is often evoked in general terms. On the whole, however, he tries to re-create and relive the feeling of each past moment, as if he did not know what lay in store. The convention of perfect memory is an obvious artifice, which readers accept so as to allow the story to be told. Closer to Camus, Gide used such a device in *The Immoralist,* a novel most of which purports to be a letter wherein a listener has written down verbatim all that the protagonist said in a nearly two-hundred-page autobiographical monologue. Camus dispenses with the contrived narrative situation and transcriber, but presents a narrative text with a similar structure.

The first chapter of *The Stranger,* where the funeral is recounted, is one of the longest in the novel. Until the prosecutor turns it into evidence of a criminal heart, Meursault's behavior seems very ordinary, but he lavishes attention on the details of his trip to Marengo. In some respects the pattern of the chapter resembles that of the chapter on the murder: both begin with moment-by-moment descriptions of apparently routine activities, both end with Meursault increasingly confused. In both the clinical precision of the early sections follows a chronological order with no obvious focus and no sign of dramatic progress. In the murder chapter, however, there is a hint of the fated encounter right at the start, and the action begins building toward a climax with the first of the three successive walks on the beach. In the first chapter, although it too ends with a walk in the hot sun, there is little sign of a climactic moment; nothing about the burial ceremony has been problematized at that point. The most suspenseful aspect would no doubt be Thomas Pérez's effort to keep pace with the procession. One might compare his disappearances and reappearances, as he takes shortcuts, to the repeated appearances of the Arab on the beach, and Pérez's collapse in a faint at the end to the Arab's collapse from the gunshot. The two figures are presented quite differently, however: as the funeral comes to an end, Meursault condenses more and more, so that Pérez's swoon appears in a long list of random images he has retained—"Then there was the church and the villagers on the sidewalks, the red geraniums on the graves in the cemetery, Pérez fainting (he crumpled like a rag doll), the blood-red earth spilling over Maman's casket, the white flesh of the roots mixed in with it, more people, voices, the village, waiting in front of a café, the incessant drone of the motor" (18; GS 22)—whereas the style grows more and more metaphorical, but no less detailed, in the passages relating the murder.

The narration of the funeral does not lack imagery; the colors, smells, and sounds are vividly conveyed. Metaphorical terms are rarer, however. When Meursault describes the patients at the Marengo home, he most often uses the same tone of detached observation that he uses for the room, the furniture, and the coffin. As he summarizes it himself, "I saw them more clearly than I had ever seen anyone, and not one detail of their faces or their clothes escaped me. But I couldn't hear them, and it was hard for me to believe they really existed" (9; GS 10). Several times he remarks on his inability to understand them: he cannot tell whether they are nodding to greet him or because of an infirmity; he has a fleeting impression that they have come to judge him; he supposes that "the dead woman lying in front of them didn't mean anything to them" (11; GS 12–13); he feels one man's eyes fixed on him, waiting for him to wake; he is surprised that they shake hands with him in the morning, "as if that night during which we hadn't exchanged as much as a single word had somehow brought us closer together" (12; GS 13).

REMEMBERING THE FUNERAL

Meursault is reconstructing a time when he did not yet understand his mother's last days, as he thinks he does in the final pages of the novel. It is noteworthy that with hindsight he corrects the supposition that the body meant nothing to them; it is one of the rare clues that the event is being told from a later moment. Nowhere is Meursault more a stranger and outsider than at his mother's funeral. Emotionally separated from her himself, he cannot share her friends' grief nor their sense of community. To him these old folks, his mother included, are like objects. They offer him neither gratification of the senses nor of the ego; his social obligations to them are a burden.

Meursault's eventual understanding of his mother must not be confused with pity or grief. As Meursault phrases it, "Nobody, nobody had the right to cry over her" (122; GS 154). Presumably this would exclude even Thomas Pérez, her "fiancé," and the sobbing friend at the wake, although it is not certain they weep for her rather than for themselves. The point is that Meursault discovers a new value to life on the very brink of death, and he thinks his mother must have made a similar discovery. During her lifetime, and still at her funeral, he did not understand. Would it have made any difference if he had? Meursault never finds any value in regret, and indeed specifically finds peace of mind in accepting all his past just as it was, including not only his callousness at the funeral but also the murder. Yet it appears that a better understanding would have affected his life for the better and he was obscurely aware of it all along.

Madame Meursault and her death haunt Meursault's thoughts throughout the novel. Upon his return to Algiers, Meursault spends an apparently carefree weekend, going swimming, taking Marie to the movies, spending the night with her, and relaxing at his window. The prosecutor, of course, makes much of this behavior, as showing hardhearted disrespect for his mother's memory. Meursault makes no effort to justify himself; he never says, for example, "Although I was behaving normally, I was thinking about her," which is what his own lawyer asks him to do. Nevertheless, at the end of the day, he does think of her: "It occurred to me that anyway one more Sunday was over, that Maman was buried now, that I was going back to work, and that, really, nothing had changed" (24; GS 30). In some respects this is a chilling remark, but it reveals his recurrent reflexion on the subject, and expresses an insight that Meursault applies eventually to his own death: the dead do not live on in the memories of the living.

Salamano and His Dog.

A few days later Meursault thinks of his mother again. Meanwhile, his boss and his friends have expressed their condolences, but these social courtesies do not awaken any real feelings in Meursault, any more than his wearing a black tie, which Marie asks him about on their first date. He replies with evasive courtesies himself, and believes that everyone is glad to change the subject. The days are relatively uneventful for Meursault; he goes to his office and sees Marie again. He also takes the first steps of his involvement with Raymond and his Arab girlfriend, and sees his neighbor Salamano. It is Salamano who reminds him of his mother, by weeping for his lost dog: "And from the peculiar little noise coming through the partition, I realized he was crying. For some reason I thought of Maman" (39; GS 50).

Salamano and his dog mirror in certain ways the relation between Meursault and his mother. Salamano tells Meursault that he got the dog as a consolation for the loss of his wife. To the outward observer Salamano despises the dog and mistreats it. The only time we see them together, the old man is cursing and beating the dog. Meursault says that they have been behaving like that for eight years; both the kindly Céleste and the brutal Raymond protest at Salamano's cruelty to his pet. But when the dog runs away, it becomes evident that Salamano felt a strong bond to it. Salamano is someone whose feelings are misunderstood by outsiders, and he is in that regard comparable to Meursault. Salamano, moreover, claims to understand Meursault's relation to his mother and defends his decision to send her to the Marengo home.

One could also say that Salamano is an old person weeping for a loss that will soon be forgotten, like Meursault's mother in her first months at the asylum. Salamano managed to replace his wife, whom he had not liked much but missed after her death, with the dog, and one can guess that he will adjust to the dog's loss, too. One of Meursault's mother's favorite maxims was that "after a while you could get used to anything" (77; GS 96). It matters very little why Salamano evokes the memory of the mother; Meursault asserts that he does not know exactly. What matters is the persistence of thoughts about the mother, apparently buried and forgotten, yet mysteriously reincarnate for Meursault in the form of Salamano and his dog. Significantly, chapters 3, 4, and 5 all end with Salamano, first the dog moaning, then Salamano weeping at his loss, and finally Salamano hoping that he will not hear other dogs barking in the night and be reminded. There is an evolution here, parallel to Meursault's relation with his mother: first their unhappy life together, then her departure and ultimately her death, and finally his unsuccessful attempts to suppress her memory.

Raymond and His Mistress. If Salamano and his dog offer one kind of parallel, Raymond and his Moorish mistress present another. Nothing in their story ever explicitly reminds Meursault of his mother. Rather, it is the fact that Raymond, Salamano, and Meursault are neighbors, and that Meursault tells their stories in alternating episodes. In many ways it is easier to explain Meursault's shooting the Arab than his participation in Raymond's sordid projects. The murder can be seen as accidental or impulsive. Writing the letter for Raymond and testifying on his behalf are both deliberate and dishonest actions, for which the Moorish woman suffers severely. Some critics gloss over this episode, describing it in euphemistic terms like "doing a simple favor for a friend." Others treat it as a blind spot in Camus's moral sensibility, a remnant of the culture in which he grew up and which he had not adequately examined. It is perhaps useful also to regard it as part of the range of flawed behaviors that Meursault adopts or observes in part 1, and understands differently at the end of part 2. Meursault's detachment from his mother, his boorishness toward Marie, Salamano's mistreatment of his dog, Raymond's beating his mistress, and finally Meursault's shooting the Arab are linked by the lack of sympathy and generosity in all five incidents. They form a scale of increasing barbarity and intolerability in a civilized society. They are all also explainable in human terms and are, if not normal, at least commonplace.

The Sun. From this perspective, the prosecutor is not wrong to connect the murder of the Arab to Meursault's conduct at the funeral. The link is further established in the language Meursault uses to describe the two events. We have seen that the sun seems to Meursault the most powerful cause of his action. It presses him onward, it blinds him, its glare becomes a flashing sword, it transforms the silence into the clash of cymbals. On his third walk on the beach, alone, after two confrontations with the Arabs, Meursault stands face to face with his adversary: "The sun was starting to burn my cheeks, and I could feel drops of sweat gathering in my eyebrows. The sun was the same as it had been the day I'd buried Maman, and like then, my forehead especially was hurting me, all the veins in it throbbing under the skin" (58–59; GS 75).

At the funeral the sun plays a less dramatic role. Nevertheless, as the procession begins, the sun is already beating down with immense power. The undertaker's man comments on it, as does the nurse. To Meursault the heat and glare dehumanize the landscape and create a dreamlike atmosphere. Because of his lack of sleep the night before, plus the heat of the day, Meursault finds it hard "to see or think straight" (17; GS 20). He makes a rather sorry contrast to old Pérez, who, despite his age and his limp, persists out of loyalty in following the procession until he collapses. His is presumably the sort of tribute to the dead one expects from the surviving loved ones.

Meursault remembers with unusual vividness what the nurse says to him; he quotes it again after his arrest. Her remark was: "If you go slowly, you risk getting sunstroke. But if you go too fast, you work up a sweat and then catch a chill inside the church." Meursault reacts at the time by thinking, "She was right. There was no way out" (17; GS 21). He recalls the comment in the second chapter of part 2, where he describes getting used to life in prison. Six months have passed, but he has little sense of the time. He observes, "Only the words 'yesterday' and 'tomorrow' still had any meaning for me" (80; GS 100). The jailor tells him he has been in prison six months, and he undergoes a sort of enlightenment. First he uses his tin plate as a mirror to study his own face; this is a classic image of self-examination, which Camus uses in several of his works. He continues studying his face as the sun sets, and suddenly becomes aware of a sound: "I distinctly heard the sound of my own voice. I recognized it as the same one that had been ringing in my ears for many long days, and I realized that all that time I had been talking to myself" (81; GS 101). Here is yet another insight into the narrative we have been reading: it is Meursault talking to himself, but partly without even being aware of it. Unlike a stream of consciousness, where impressions and memories are freely associated and jumbled together, Meursault's voice is very rational, articulate, and clear. But as he describes it, it speaks to his conscious mind from some other level of awareness, where he might have unexpected insights. It is in the conclusion of this scene that he relates: "Then I remembered what the nurse at Maman's funeral said. No, there was no way out, and no one can imagine what nights in prison are like" (81; GS 101).

Sleep. Meursault's goal on the beach, as at the funeral, is to find peace and quiet. On the beach he thinks of the fountain, "the cool spring behind the rock . . . shade and rest" (57; GS 73). At the end of the funeral he thinks he will "go to bed and sleep for twelve hours" (18; GS 22). Sleep is probably his most consistent drive throughout the novel. He sleeps on the bus going to Marengo, he dozes during the wake, he longs to sleep back in Algiers. Marie leaves while he is still asleep their first night together, and she has to shake him to awaken him the day they go to the beach. He naps during his lunch hour and ends several chapters by noting that he went to bed. He dozes during his trial as he had during the funeral. In his first days in jail, sleep was a problem, but he succeeded gradually in sleeping "sixteen to eighteen hours a day" (79; GS 99). After his outburst against the chaplain, he falls asleep exhausted. One of the most beautiful sentences in the novel concludes chapter 3 of part 2, as Meursault returns to prison from the courtroom on a summer evening and hears familiar sounds, and thinks: "Familiar paths traced in summer skies could lead as easily to prison as to the sleep of the innocent" (97; GS 123). "Easy, dreamless sleep," as he calls it in the same passage, seems to Meursault the sign of contentment with life.

Sleep is, however, also a sign of indifference and irresponsibility. Almost the first obligation expected of Meursault in *The Stranger* is to remain awake for a night beside his mother's coffin. He has great difficulty doing so, and in fact dozes. He wakens briefly and sees one old man "staring at me as if he were just waiting for me to wake up" (11; GS 13). In the metaphorical sense, Meursault does not awaken until the final scene of the novel. As we have already observed, the group of patients who join Meursault in the vigil disturb him. When they first arrive, he notes, "For a second I had the ridiculous feeling that they were there to judge me" (10; GS 11). Perhaps it was not so ridiculous; Meursault comes back repeatedly to the theme of his guilt, just as he does to the memory of his mother.

The Gaze of Others. Even before the funeral, he finds himself saying to his boss, "It's not my fault" (3; GS 1). Thinking it over, he concludes that he had no need to say it. Nonetheless he repeats it to himself, to justify getting four days off from work: "It isn't my fault if they buried Maman yesterday instead of today" (19; GS 22). And the impulse strikes him again with Marie: "I felt like telling her it wasn't my fault, but I stopped myself because I remembered that I'd already said that to my boss. It didn't mean anything. Besides, you always feel a little guilty" (20; GS 24). These small pangs of a vague guilt echo the insight of the wake: Meursault is being judged all the time, whether he is always aware of it or not. Moreover, as he lets slip in a passing comment, he always feels guilty.

As the trial gets under way, Meursault confronts a real jury. Like the old man at the wake, "they were all looking at me" (83; GS 103). And like the old people as a group, "I can't say what distinguished one from another. I had just one impression: I was sitting across from a row of seats on a streetcar and all these anonymous passengers were looking over the new arrival to see if they could find something funny about him. I knew it was a silly idea since it wasn't anything funny they were after but a crime. There isn't much difference, though" (83; GS 103–4). Meursault rides a number of trams and busses in *The Stranger,* although without ever commenting on this feeling. It is more to the point that he himself has a keen eye for ridiculous traits, and notices about the Marengo patients the skinny men, the "bulging

stomachs" of the women (10; GS 11), their nests of wrinkles, the awkward wagging of their heads, the sucking of their lips, and their tooth-
less gums. At Marengo he also records the nurse whose nose has been
eaten away by an abscess and Thomas Pérez with a pimply nose and
floppy red ears. Back in Algiers, he spots the caricatural family in their
Sunday best and the strange little robot woman with a face like an
apple; even his portraits of friends, like the paunchy Céleste and the
ungainly Salamano with thin hair and a blotchy complexion, are none
too flattering.

Meursault gazes a lot at others; until the trial, he is only occasionally conscious of being gazed at, but then it arouses his sense of
guilt. At the trial he first notices the stares of the jurors, but soon feels
the young journalist's "two very bright eyes, which were examining
me closely" (85; GS 107) and the robot woman "staring right at me"
(86; GS 108) as well. Meursault is insistent about them: "The young
reporter and the little robot woman were still there. They weren't fan-
ning themselves, but they were still watching me without saying a
word" (88–89; GS 109); "My eyes met those of the little robot woman
and the reporter in the gray jacket" (105; GS 133). The looks he gets
from these people are not always hostile; Meursault thinks he detects
sympathy in the journalist and respect from everyone present when he
is sentenced. The witnesses also look at him, the caretaker in gratitude,
Céleste in apology, Raymond in affirmation of friendship. Marie apparently watches him sympathetically during the whole proceeding,
although he looks at her only once near the end.

One of the most important gazes to fall on Meursault comes from
his victim. As Raymond, Marie, and Meursault set out for the beach,
Raymond calls Meursault's attention to a group of Arabs across the
street: "They were staring at us in silence, but in that way of theirs, as
if we were nothing but stones or dead trees" (48; GS 61). This reifying
stare may recall Meursault's aloof commentary on his mother's mour-
ners. As the confrontations begin, the staring contest intensifies. On
the second meeting the two Arabs face the two Europeans: "We stared
at each other, without blinking" (56; GS 72). But this time the Arabs
slip away. The third time Meursault goes alone and finds his victim

alone; once again their eyes fix on each other. This time Meursault notes, "Maybe it was the shadows on his face, but it looked like he was laughing" (58; GS 75). This laugh, which may never have existed, recalls the passengers on the tramway, examining and judging the newcomer. It also looks forward in Camus's works to *The Fall,* where a ghostly laugh shatters the narrator's complacently self-righteous opinion of himself. In *The Stranger,* too, the laugh has mysterious origins; it may be as much the work of shadows, of the sun, of nature, as of a person. Hearing that laugh, Meursault feels guilty.

In his prison cell he finds a second crucial gaze, his own. After six months pass of which he was barely aware—"For me it was one and the same unending day that was unfolding in my cell and the same thing I was trying to do" (80; GS 101)—Meursault looks at his reflection in his tin plate. What he sees does not surprise him; he has a serious expression, but he has been feeling serious. More surprisingly, the experience makes him aware of his own voice, which has been sounding in his ears: "I realized that all that time I had been talking to myself" (81; GS 101). This self-knowledge also brings back into his thoughts a memory of the funeral, the nurse's remark that "there was no way out" (81; GS 101). This revelation occurs only halfway through part 2; Meursault must still submit to the judgment of the court and to the confrontation with the chaplain. Here, however, he begins to change; this mirror reflects a step toward understanding, unlike a mirror in part 1, in which he saw reflected meaningless objects—a corner of his table with his alcohol lamp and some bits of bread beside it—inspiring the thought: "It occurred to me that anyway one more Sunday was over, that Maman was buried now, and that I was going back to work, and that, really, nothing had changed" (24; GS 30).

Finally, Meursault must face the chaplain's gaze. "At that he stood up and looked me straight in the eye. It was a game I knew well. I played it a lot with Emmanuel and Céleste and usually they were the ones who looked away. The chaplain knew the game well too, I could tell right away; his gaze never faltered" (117; GS 147). Meursault wins the contest all the same, when he answers the questions "Have you no hope at all? And do you really live with the thought that when you die, you die, and nothing remains?" with a blunt "Yes" (117; GS 147). Meursault is on the verge of a liberating outburst against the chaplain. He has reconstructed the story of how that outburst came about; from a passive and ultimately culpable immersion in the present, he has been compelled to think himself. The force that drove him to this painful task has been guilt, in part a legal guilt for murder that deprives him of all illusions of freedom, and in part a vague sense of responsibility that leads him to evasions, to resistance, and finally to murder.

GUILT

In the final pages of the novel this obscure intuition of guilt explodes into a declaration of universal human guilt. In his rage against the chaplain he says, "The others would all be condemned one day. And he would be condemned, too. What would it matter if he were accused of murder and then executed because he didn't cry at his mother's funeral? Salamano's dog was worth just as much as his wife. The little robot woman was just as guilty as the Parisian woman Masson married, or as Marie, who had wanted me to marry her" (121; GS 152). One might describe *The Stranger* as the story of Meursault's understanding his guilt. In that final revelation he breaks loose almost for the only time, from his careful notation of his own thoughts and feelings as purely individual and circumstantial facts, to speak of general truths.

The Stranger relates a progress toward understanding. The Meursault of part 1 never thinks seriously about himself; he lives in the present, contented and unconcerned. His apathy contains a fatal flaw, however, which lets him fall into the trap of circumstances and turns him into a murderer. Once this has happened, he is forced by his trial to hear himself interpreted. Meanings are ascribed to his actions and to his life. He rejects them, but still has nothing to put in their place. Neither the trial nor prison affects him intellectually; his apathy protects him even there, and he defeats punishment by adapting to it.

At the very end the chaplain shakes him from his apathy. In the next chapter we consider what new elements finally transform Meursault. For his story to have its effect, however, we must pass through his life as he has lived it. That is to say, the understanding he acquires at the end is not a philosophical principle that can be stated and learned, but an experience. Meursault poses the problem in a radical form; his apathy is more total than one finds outside fiction, his resistance to meaning is more stubborn. Neither he nor his life is intended to be realistic; *The Stranger* is something more like a parable. Part of what it teaches is a necessity of rereading. Only in the last pages does Meursault himself understand what has gone before; he then rereads his life. As narrator, he reconstructs his past to enable the reader to follow the same circular course, using the key of the final pages.

MEURSAULT'S FINAL THOUGHTS

ON THE EDGE OF DEATH

The Stranger tells the story of a man who has drifted through life. He has apparently shunned all temptations and pressures to give his life a direction. Neither stupid nor unperceptive, he usually knows what other people expect of him, and within limits he gives it. Yet he stubbornly resists expressing his own feelings in meaningful terms, that is, in terms that imply a relation to other people. Nonetheless, he allows others to act as if the relationship existed and even performs the duties it implies. Through apathy he has wandered into a career without ambition, into an engagement without love, into a friendship without affection, and into a quarrel without anger. For the murder he is brought to trial, and in court he begins to act like a stranger or outsider. That is, even though his life now depends on it, he will not profess feelings he did not or does not have. It seems clear that, in Camus's opinion, this stubbornness is a genuine heroism: Meursault reveals an admirable passion for truth, and through his passion, we may be enlightened. Yet it also seems clear that, by itself, a passion for truth is not enough to live by. It may have been better to hurt Marie's feelings than to pretend to love her, but this brutal sincerity did not signify that Meursault possessed a full moral consciousness of what was happening. We must ask ourselves what sort of world is revealed by Meursault's scrupulous adherence to truth. Meursault himself seems to reach a new level of understanding at the very end, suggesting that something was amiss theretofore.

Moreover, we cannot tolerate his actions, either. If the only way to emulate Meursault were to commit murder, his moral example would be repugnant. Somewhere in Meursault's final illumination, Camus must give us insight into the fallacy in his attitude that led him so thoughtlessly to take another person's life. As we have observed, Meursault's reflections turn far more often to his mother's death than to any of his other actions. He never really expresses any feeling about killing the Arab. In a sense, remorse would be superfluous; Meursault knew the moment he did it that he had done wrong. No reader should need to be told that murder is bad. After the outburst against the chaplain, Camus does not fill Meursault's mind with clichés about the horror of ending another man's life; rather, he looks toward a more subtle and more commonplace problem: a sympathetic understanding of the mother's final days. There appears to be something like a moral teaching implicit in Meursault's last thoughts, but its focus comes as a surprise and requires a closer look. Meursault's conscience is plagued less by his obvious crime than by his secret failings.

The inescapable fact that Meursault confronts at the end of *The Stranger* is death. He screams at the chaplain that he is "sure of my life and sure of the death I had waiting for me" (120; GS 151), and while that certainty might seem like a small verity, Meursault comes to regard it as more significant than anything else. In his rage at the chaplain, he grows eloquent in stating that death comes to everyone:

> Throughout the whole absurd life I'd lived, a dark wind had been rising toward me from somewhere deep in my future, across years that were still to come, and as it passed, this wind leveled whatever was offered to me at the time, in years no more real than the ones I was living. What did other people's deaths or a mother's love matter to me; what did his God or the lives people choose or the fate they think they elect matter to me when we're all elected by the same fate, me and billions of privileged people like him who also

called themselves my brothers? Couldn't he see, couldn't he see that? Everybody was privileged. There were only privileged people. The others would all be condemned one day. And he would be condemned, too. What would it matter if he were accused of murder and then executed because he didn't cry at his mother's funeral? (121; GS 152)

We have looked at some of these lines before, and emphasized the implication of universal guilt: everyone is *condemned*. As the whole passage makes evident, however, the universality of the punishment makes the guilt meaningless. As Meursault asks, what difference does it make how anyone lives, since everyone is condemned to die in any case? We seem to be thrown back upon the principle of Meursault's life before the murder: the sole value one possesses is the present moment, every act is equal to every other act.

THE CHAPLAIN

The priest arrives at the novel's climax to provoke the lethargic Meursault into vehement response, because he represents the sternest challenge to Meursault's position. He has often been taken for a contemptible character. His pursuit of the reluctant Meursault, his offensive cocksureness, and his rejection by Meursault seem to mark him as a negative force, allied with hypocritical oppressors like the prosecutor and the judge. In particular, his appearance closes part 2 on the same note that it began, with the magistrate thrusting a crucifix at Meursault and pressuring him to confess his faith in God. It is true that the priest also forces himself on Meursault and badgers him with questions until Meursault loses his temper; but he leaves with dignity. He has asked Meursault the right questions. He has forced the silent outsider to articulate his thoughts. He has awakened the sleeper to a rush of vital energy. He has endowed the irresponsible apathetic criminal with a moral consciousness. It is the priest who transforms Meursault into a possible hero.

Similarities to Meursault. The priest and Meursault sound as though they agree on many points. Before Meursault's tirade the chaplain had said that "the way he saw it, we were all condemned to die" (117; GS 146), concurring not only in the universal but also in the punitive nature of death. Both believe in the meaninglessness of the life here below; for the man of faith, only God's judgment matters. Meursault, of course, objects and makes distinctions; he does not share the chaplain's belief that his sins and crimes could be abolished by a sincere repentance, or that this life is insignificant by comparison to the eternal life. In fact, he does not recognize the idea of sin, and talks of the crime as a contractual matter, in which the penalty pays off the debt incurred in the act. The two men share a certain conception of earthly reality as transitory and imperfect. But the chaplain resolves the moral problems raised by this conception with the belief that a divine order transcends the confusing turmoil of earthly existence. As a clergyman in an organized church, he also claims some knowledge of that divine order, and he urges Meursault to have faith in it, too.

Despite Meursault's violent reaction, the chaplain leaves with a gesture of apparent sympathy. Meursault's assault causes the guards to rush into the cell; they free the chaplain and threaten to strike Meursault. "He calmed them, though, and looked at me for a moment without saying anything. His eyes were full of tears. Then he turned and disappeared" (122; GS 153). The chaplain appears to have understood Meursault's point. His tears recall those of other sympathetic figures, like Céleste at the trial. Tears are the sign of someone's feeling that words have proven inadequate to the expression of human truth. Marie breaks down on the witness stand and sobs incoherently that the prosecutor had made her "say the opposite of what she was thinking" (94; GS 118). Salamano weeps for his lost dog; on the witness stand he appeals pathetically, "You must understand," but as Meursault notes sardonically, "no one seemed to understand" (95; GS 118), and like Marie he is led away.

Religion in Camus. For Meursault's greatest offense was not the murder so much as the thoughtlessness that lay behind it, and the same thoughtlessness also lay behind his other actions, good and bad, admirable or despicable, ordinary or bizarre. Meursault has a raw intuition of what Camus called "the absurd." As Sartre was the first to point out, Camus developed the same ideas in another work published the same year as *The Stranger,* a philosophical essay entitled *The Myth of Sisyphus. The Myth of Sisyphus* traces the history of the idea of the absurd among philosophers and writers; it discusses several mythic figures, like Don Juan, as heroes of the absurd; it analyzes its implications for moral conduct. It is, in short, a work addressed to intellectuals who want to reason about the absurd. *The Stranger,* on the other hand, tries to convey the immediate apprehension of the absurd in human existence.

Camus remained firm throughout his life in a position of agnosticism; he did not believe in a god of any sort. He nonetheless maintained a constant dialogue with religious, and especially Christian, moral philosophers. *The Myth of Sisyphus* devotes a great deal of attention to the Christian existentialists, who share many ideas with him; Camus parts company with them only in their final leap of faith. It was Camus himself who called Meursault a Christ figure, however paradoxically he meant it. In *The Plague* another priest, Father Paneloux, is one of the central characters, articulating an absolutely consistent religious attitude toward natural evil. *The Fall* takes its title in part from the biblical story of Adam, and is full of Christian allusions. *Exile and the Kingdom* is likewise permeated with Christian images and symbols, including the metaphor of the title. It should therefore be no surprise that a Christian challenge prods Meursault into thinking through his own belief and stating his defense.

MEURSAULT AND INTERPRETATION

Meursault finds problems of interpretation everywhere; his very first lines depict him wondering what the telegram means. In a practical sense he copes well enough most of the time. Meaning for him never seems to go beyond a sort of consensual agreement, however. He has a notion of what the Marengo staff expects of him, and of what his boss, his friends, Marie, Raymond, the magistrate, his defense lawyer, and almost everyone else expect of him. Most of the time he tries to please them, as when he promises his lawyer not to repeat his remark that "all normal people have wished their loved ones were dead" (65; GS 80). Meursault tries to explain, but the lawyer leaves still unsatisfied; Meursault wishes "I could have made him stay, to explain that I wanted things between us to be good, not so that he'd defend me better but, if I can put it this way, good in a natural way" (65–66; GS 81). Meursault will not play the hypocrite for an obvious personal gain, but he trades promises and actions for the immediate quid pro quo of being liked. Yet he remains incapable of any long-term subordination of his attitudes and feelings, that is, of his innermost self, to some ultimate purpose. The borderline between an immediate reward and a meaningful purpose remains vague and no doubt fluctuates; there is no systematic distinction to be made. The point is rather that Meursault sees almost nothing in terms of a broad purpose. Given the choice, he adopts a local and short-term explanation in preference to a broader one.

In this exchange Meursault realizes that his lawyer "didn't understand me, and he was sort of holding it against me. I felt the urge to reassure him that I was like everybody else, just like everybody else. But really there wasn't much point, and I gave up the idea out of laziness" (66; GS 81). To know whether or not the effort served a purpose would require Meursault to think hard about his purposes. Typically, he dismisses the idea out of hand. He prefers the handy explanation of laziness to a broader claim involving purpose. He is, of course, at least partly right to blame laziness, but he appears to mean only the physical fatigue that he so often succumbs to. That is in a sense only the symptom of a worse malady, a spiritual laziness. Even at the end Meursault would have certainly persisted in the idea he expressed earlier, that it would serve no great purpose to win the lawyer's friendship. At the end, however, Meursault has recognized the implications of denying purpose.

Meursault acknowledges in this discussion that he understands the desire to make sense of things—of his own character, in this case. He admits that it is natural to be irritated by the lack of sense. This desire for meaning is implicit in many of Meursault's remarks; he often tries to interpret things, or catches himself interpreting, as at the funeral. His very refusal to use a few terms casually, such as *love* or *regret*, implies an intense concern about meanings. If nothing really mattered, it would not matter if he pretended that it did. But pretense does matter to Meursault, at least in some situations, and it matters so much that he allows himself to be sentenced to death rather than pretend to be other than he is.

The Absurd. In *The Myth of Sisyphus* Camus makes clear that the absurd arises from the contact of two elements: the absence of meaning in the natural world, and the desire for meaning in human beings. The mere fact of randomness or chaos by itself is not absurd. The absurd is born only when randomness or chaos is confronted with the human need for order, interpretation, and meaning. Meursault would not be a hero of the absurd if he felt no hunger for meaning; he would be instead a thing, like a stone, in one of Camus's favorite images. Meursault does feel that hunger, however, and if at times he seems not to, it is because he has repressed and silenced its cry within himself. After disappointing his boss by his lack of ambition, he tells us that he used to be ambitious until he was forced to abandon his studies. In the conversation with the defense lawyer he says that "I had pretty much lost the habit of analyzing myself" (65; GS 80), as if in an earlier time he had analyzed himself more intently. Since his feelings are the most frequent pretexts for his denials of meaning and significance, this hint of a previous state is highly suggestive. Meursault may be more an exile than a stranger, someone who has lost his sense of belonging rather than someone who never belonged.

The Denial of Meaning. Whatever the traumatic cause of his alienation, he has remained in a state of only partial enlightenment. He has rejected the commonplace and facile solution of accepting the readiest meaning because it is easy, consoling, satisfying—that is, because it assuages the universal human desire. *The Stranger* is full of small examples of such hypocrisies and compromises. We have already seen the principal examples in his refusal to feign filial grief at the funeral, professional ambition with his boss, or love with Marie. In each case the public expects a behavior in accord with widely held values, implying a mystical blood tie between parent and child, a sense of purpose or destiny in one's life, a spiritual exaltation through sexual union. Those who most directly express these expectations to Meursault are not necessarily his enemies, either: the goodhearted Céleste surely tries to say something of the sort in his hackneyed comment "You only have one mother" (3–4; GS 2); the boss is offering an opportunity for advancement; and Marie says she loves Meursault even though he will not say he loves her.

If circumstances had not led him to commit the murder, Meursault might have lived out his days as a somewhat churlish loner. His inability to find any purpose in life, or his unwillingness to accept any of the purposes he sees, bring harm chiefly to him. In Camus's last published work, the book of short stories *Exile and the Kingdom,* one finds a character who could almost be Meursault grown old: the husband, Marcel, in the story "The Adulterous Woman." Married but childless, he depends on his wife Janine for sex but nothing else; they have virtually nothing to say to each other. Janine, who could be Marie grown older, a bit overweight and short of breath, has accompanied Marcel on a sales trip to a desert village. She remembers their youth, especially trips to the beach, and their dreams of comfort, shattered by the war. At first devastated by the realization that nothing has turned out as she had hoped, she experiences an ambiguous but apparently liberating ecstasy in contemplating the desert, the nomads, and especially the night sky. She, too, seems to conclude that life has no meaning, but having reached that point of despair she has an illumination that resembles Meursault's.

The Role of Chance. Chance, however, propels Meursault toward an earlier confrontation with the absurd. His nonchalant reluctance to make judgments leads him into a dangerous friendship with Raymond. His assumption that all actions are the same leads him to go back to the beach a third time. His refusal to attach any importance to plans or purposes makes the capital crime of murder indistinguishable from a walk in the sun or a drink in the shade. Meursault has followed the consequences of his perception of meaninglessness all the way to nihilism. Meursault is no intellectual; he did not learn nihilism from reading philosophy, or adopt it as an ideology. Rather he slid into it through passivity. His response to his inability to find meaning has been a form of egotism. He cares only for his sensual pleasures and creature comforts. Meursault resembles an animal in many ways, existing only to eat, sleep, and bask, slipping into a sheltering crevice whenever his tranquillity is threatened. Even at the end, he tries to withdraw into the seclusion of his cell to escape the prying queries of the chaplain.

It is an inextricable mixture of chance and negligence that leads to the murder. Meursault and his friends seem comic at the trial, blaming the shooting on chance. Yet we are assured by Meursault's narrative that he had no intentions, good or bad. How then could he have intended the murder? He could, however, have prevented it; but to do so, he would have needed some principle of conduct, some standard of value, some reason to care. As soon as the deed is done, Meursault himself realizes that he has transgressed. He knows it, not because of any sudden pity for his victim, but because of the realization that he has destroyed his own peace. He puts it in symbolic terms: "I knew that I had shattered the harmony of the day, the exceptional silence of a beach where I'd been happy" (59; GS 76). He has much still to understand; as he says himself, the first shot is when "it all started." The moral lesson of the first half of *The Stranger* is almost what the prosecutor claims: that a man who does not cry at his mother's funeral is already a criminal at heart. Meursault has no criminal intentions, but he has no intention to avoid crime, either. Yet his profound reason for not crying, his perception of the truth and his allegiance to that truth, seem irrefutable. Camus's task in the second half of *The Stranger* is to let Meursault understand what was lacking in his view of the world. The accidental murder starts him on the road to that knowledge.

Resistance to Change. The chronicle of Meursault's first six months in jail gives no indication of a change in spirit. Nothing suggests that he ever thinks of his crime, although presumably he discusses it with his lawyer, who visits occasionally. All that concerns Meursault, however, is the painful transition from having the thoughts "of a free man" to having "those of a prisoner" (76–77; GS 95). It takes only a few months. Meursault thinks that even if he "had had to live in the trunk of a dead tree," he would have "gotten used to it" (77; GS 95). For a person who sees no meaning in things, one kind of life may be more pleasant than another. But even though one follows the other, there is no meaningful connection between them. In the physical world Meursault comprehends that some actions cause certain results, and sometimes he seems to grasp simple causes in human relations, but not always. He never seems to make a moral connection. He deduces that he is being punished through logical processes or because the jailor tells him; the punishment itself never means anything to him.

The trial has no more impact on him. He watches the trial with the same detached and intermittent curiosity that he brought to the funeral. Details catch his eye but he cannot master the whole procedure as a meaningful event. Indeed, he finds the prosecutor's closing argument barely distinguishable from his own lawyer's, he loses the thread of both, gets bored with them and stops listening. He finds his own interrogation repetitive and pointless, and gives an incoherent account of it. He pays more attention to his friends Céleste, Marie, Salamano, Masson, and Raymond when they testify, but he only sketches the testimony of the hostile witnesses. Moreover, when Meursault is tempted to intervene, he usually damages his own case, as when he confirms that he offered the caretaker a cigarette. Meursault does not understand what either of the lawyers is trying to prove; his main feeling is that "Everything was happening without my participation" (98; GS 124). Ultimately, he more or less accedes to his exclusion. Even the verdict comes across simply as "bizarre language" (107; GS 135).

THE FINAL ILLUMINATION

In short, whatever it is that Meursault learns before the end of the novel, whatever it is that prompts him to feel that on the eve of his execution he is "ready to live it all again" and that his feeling then is new, "for the first time" (122; GS 154), it comes to him all at once because of the chaplain's intervention. He relives and reinterprets his past, and, of course, his memories supply the material for his conclusions. But as he retells it, no glimmer of revelation reached him while that past was in progress. The Meursault of the last paragraph is an entirely new Meursault. But what can have changed?

The Abandonment of Hope. Paradoxically, he has given up hope. Yet hope was a relatively recent element in his makeup. Before his conviction, he entertained few hopes, seeming indifferent to his future with Marie, for example, or even the chance of winning his case. He had been equally apathetic before the murder, showing no ambition and no strong desires. After the conviction, however, he becomes preoccupied with "escaping the machinery of justice, seeing if there's any way out of the inevitable" (108; GS 136); that is, is there any way to escape the guillotine? "What really counted was the possibility of escape, a leap to freedom, out of the implacable ritual, a wild run for it that would give whatever chance for hope there was" (109; GS 137). His best hope, of course, is his appeal, which remains an open question. He thinks about it, obsessively, but as he relates his thoughts, he never mulls over the content, only the outcome. His thought is a ritual itself; he has to begin by supposing that he loses, and accept that possibility, before he gives himself "the right . . . to consider the alternative hypothesis" (114; GS 143). Then he must restrain his joy, so as not to undermine his acceptance of failure, and when he has succeeded, he has earned "an hour of calm" (115; GS 144).

Meursault has, in effect, abstracted the question of his death from the judicial procedure. Where one might expect him to imagine strategies for the appeal—a new lawyer, a new witness, a new argument, or a new attitude of remorse on his own part—instead he treats his execution as the result of a gamble that is always lost. He dreams of reforming the system to give the victim one chance in a thousand: "the trouble with the guillotine was that you had no chance at all, absolutely none. The fact was that it had been decided once and for all that the patient was to die. It was an open-and-shut case" (111; GS 139). Moreover, just as he had attributed his crime to chance, so too he regards his impending execution as a product of chance: "The fact that the sentence had been read at eight o'clock at night and not at five o'clock, the fact that it could have been an entirely different one, the fact that it had been decided by men who change their underwear" (109; GS 137). As always, Meursault cannot comprehend the causal relations that give most people the impression that they influence if not control their lives; he still apparently cannot see the connection between his shooting the Arab, his unwillingness to express remorse, and his condemnation as a hardened killer. But that is because for Meursault, and for Camus, the essential point is not why one is condemned, because everyone is condemned.

Meursault tries this line of reasoning on himself, when he supposes that his appeal will fail: "Deep down I knew perfectly well that it doesn't much matter whether you die at thirty or at seventy, since in either case other men and women will naturally go on living—and for thousands of years. . . . Since we're all going to die, it's obvious that when and how don't matter" (114; GS 143). He has a difficult time forcing himself to follow through on that argument. It does not console him for the years of life he will lose, and in fact serves only to give him the right to contemplate the opposite: winning the appeal. In other words, he acknowledges the inevitability of death in order to have the right to hope.

Hope is what he must sacrifice, however. Hope obsesses and deludes; it obliterates the present life, the only one Meursault or anyone else possesses, in the name of some vague and illusionary future. When the chaplain proposes to him the hope of an afterlife he explodes, and the outburst of rage purges him of all hope, leaving him free to live in the certainties of the here and now.

Having given up hope, however, Meursault feels ready to begin life all over again. Moreover, he understands for the first time why his mother, in the home at Marengo, should have "played at beginning again" by taking on a fiancé (122; GS 153–54). In a sense Meursault has discovered a piece of wisdom he apparently already knew: to live for the present. It was precisely because his mother no longer had to worry about whether her fiancé would ever really marry her, whether the marriage made sense or not, whether anyone else would approve, that she was free to be engaged. As he lies in his cell thinking, Meursault hears the sirens from the harbor, "announcing departures for a world that now and forever meant nothing to me" (122; GS 153). This lack of concern is a freedom. It allows Meursault to be, as he howls at the chaplain, "sure of my life and sure of the death I had waiting for me" (120; GS 151).

The Indifference of the World. In this newly found state of peace, Meursault also realizes a truth that has been implicit throughout the narrative: "the gentle indifference of the world" he calls it. Furthermore he discovers a kinship between it and himself: "Finding it so much like myself—so like a brother, really—I felt that I had been happy and that I was happy again" (122–23; GS 154). Happiness is a certain harmony between the individual and nature. Meursault's unwillingness to invent meanings has indeed been a fidelity to nature. Far from suffering from the diminished status of humanity, not created by God or beloved by Him, as in a religious view, for example, Meursault finds the indifferent universe benign and fraternal. It guarantees a certain freedom.

Camus was fascinated by the idea of characters who tried to imitate the ways of the universe. The most powerful is the Roman emperor in the play *Caligula*. Known in history as an insane tyrant, Caligula becomes in Camus's hands a man who encounters the absurd through the loss of a loved one, his sister and mistress Drusilla. Caligula also happens to hold the power to do anything physically possible to human beings. He embarks on an orgy of killing and wanton mischief, in imitation of the natural universe. His subjects murmur but continue blindly to believe in the emperor's divinity, in the triumph of justice, in political order, and in similar consoling faiths. Finally they rebel and kill him, but he realizes as he dies that his method has neither made him happy himself nor forced his subjects to face the truth.

Caligula and Meursault have much in common, beginning with the fact that both are murderers presented as literary heroes. Both works begin with the natural death of another person and both end with the execution of the protagonist. Both central characters also realize at the end that they have miscalculated or misunderstood something, even though Camus has made their arguments and points of view dominant. Their final illumination reflects a subtle modification, not a radical conversion. They have been close to the truth all along, but missing a crucial element.

For Meursault that element seems to be chiefly a matter of awareness—awareness first of the value of life, and second of solidarity among those who share it. In the situation that most people would regard as the worst possible human predicament, facing imminent execution for murder, Meursault proclaims himself happy. Camus has, it would seem, designed the story so as to place Meursault in just this position, in order to give his happiness its fullest significance. If he can be happy, anyone can be. His happiness consists entirely of an inner state, in which he has finally understood his freedom and appreciated his possession of it. Obviously, it is a metaphysical freedom, not a social or political freedom. He cannot go where he wants or even do simple things like smoke a cigarette. It is a freedom that comes from affirming his own life over any life that might have been.

Meursault's life is, of course, not admirable, but its content should not matter. Camus did not by any means think that his readers ought to refuse to mourn dead parents and still less that they should murder someone. The point is really that one can affirm even a life like Meursault's—not only that one can, but one must affirm it, if one has led such a life. The path to happiness and wisdom that Camus traced depends on an unflinching acceptance of truth. Part of that truth is the indifference of the external world; another part is one's own past. To affirm one's past, however, does not imply that one remains bound by it, quite the contrary. By taking full responsibility for it, one makes the crucial last move into freedom.

Awakening to Human Solidarity. With the awareness of his own happiness comes Meursault's first sympathy for another person. He has, of course, many times understood, in a rational sense, the ideas and feelings of others. He can follow arguments and foresee reactions. But he never appears to share them, to enter into the other person's existence. In his last monologue he expresses such sympathy for his mother, whose last days he understands in a way he did not during her life or at the funeral. This is quite different from pity or feeling sorry for her; he insists that "nobody had the right to cry over her" (122; GS 154) because she too, he thinks, had discovered this freedom and the happiness it brings. And for the first time Meursault expresses a longing for human companionship: "For everything to be consummated, for me to feel less alone . . ." (123; GS 154). In his freedom he finds an impulse to solidarity.

His last wish is one of the most puzzling paradoxes of the novel: "I had only to wish that there be a large crowd of spectators the day of my execution and that they greet me with cries of hate" (123; GS 154). It is useful to recall once again Caligula, who had tried to drive his subjects into a revolt against death. Meursault has neither the demented intellect nor the imperial power to conceive such a project, but he will die for his refusal of human solidarity. The crowd will hate him not simply as a murderer, but as a cold-blooded murderer, and the difference is critical. He condemns himself, in a sense, for failing to respect life and the living.

Yet a strange phenomenon should occur at the execution. Meursault has recalled the story his mother told him of his father, who attended a public guillotining and was nauseated afterwards. Meursault, who had not appreciated the story at the time, now thinks that "there was nothing more important than an execution, and that when you come right down to it, it was the only thing a man could truly be interested in" (110; GS 138). If the scenario Meursault has traced comes to pass, then the howling mob will encounter their own mortality. Like Meursault's father (and Camus's, for the story is based on a real incident), they will see themselves in the victim, not in the impersonal entity of "the French people." They will be overwhelmed with an unanticipated sympathy that will force them to recognize their universal human solidarity.

The spiritual awakening that comes to Meursault alters his consciouness, but it remains a private and internal revolution. It affirms the value of life as it is, not life as it should be, still less as it will be in the hereafter. It proclaims the heroic courage needed to see that distinction clearly and to live in accordance with that painful truth. Most people try to evade the knowledge that this life is all they have; to hide from a painful awareness that they are allowing it to be wasted, they surrender their freedom to ready-made systems of meaning. Sartre called such evasions "bad faith," but he appeared to conclude that one must consciously commit oneself to action, whereas Camus stressed the endless need to live in full awareness of the absurd. The past cannot be undone or forgotten; as Meursault accepts the life he has led, so must everyone.

TRAGIC LONELINESS

One consequence of Camus's ethic of the absurd is a tragic loneliness. His heroes, like Meursault, are strangers, outsiders, aliens, and exiles. The bonds forged by unity in a cause, which Camus knew in his own life and which fellow writers like Sartre and Malraux celebrated, seemed to him fragile and flawed. Meursault never indicates any feelings of group solidarity, but in *The Plague* a group of solitary men unite in common cause against the deadly epidemic. The union does not survive the end of the plague, however; some die, some depart, some return to their lonely routines. Tarrou, a kind of Camusian saint, tells of his futile lifelong struggle to be, if not a good man, at least an innocent murderer. He welcomes the bubonic plague as an adversary, even though it finally kills him; he can fight against it with no qualms, unlike his earlier political enemies. In Camus's universe moments of human solidarity are rare and fleeting; Meursault's sensation of a fraternal indifference in the world is the first of many such incidents in Camus's works.

Several of Camus's characters are, like Meursault, literally murderers; we have looked at those of *Caligula* and *The Misunderstanding*. In addition, in Camus's first novel, *A Happy Death*, written before *The Stranger* but not published until 1971, a character named Patrice Mersault kills a rich cripple named Roland Zagreus to get his money. In *The Just Assassins*, the Russian terrorists plan and carry out a political assassination. In "The Renegade" a missionary, driven mad by torture and enslavement, shoots another priest who was coming on a mission to the Taghasans. *Caligula* and *The Just Assassins* are based on historical figures; they show that Camus was drawn to the study of murder, especially in extreme and exemplary situations. The other works, by contrast, turn rather ordinary and unexpected characters into murderers, as if taking the lives of others were a commonplace human activity.

In the 1930s, 1940s, and 1950s, when Camus lived and wrote, one might have said that indeed killing was a commonplace human activity, but Camus's works consistently avoid contemporary political contexts. His ideological assassins come from the past and often seem to live in mythic or allegorical worlds. When characters who seem real and close to us kill, they do so from impulse or private compulsions, never from the rationalized savagery of twentieth-century mass political movements. While fascism or communism, colonialist or liberationist terrorism may well have influenced Camus's reflections on murder, he quite obviously took great care to generalize his thought. It seems likely, in fact, that he first turned to the subject for personal reasons, confronting the possibility of his own early death from tuberculosis. *A Happy Death* makes perfect sense as the meditation of a young man without money, expecting to die soon, who wonders why he should not do whatever is necessary to enjoy his last days to the fullest. What punishment worse than death could he incur? For one who does not believe in divine law, what moral force could deter him?

In *A Happy Death* it is not possession of Zagreus's money that makes Mersault happy, but rather his deathbed affirmation of the value of his life, including his crime. In this scene especially he resembles Meursault: "Of all the men he had carried within himself like everyone at the start of life, of these various beings who mixed their roots without confusing them, he knew now which one he had been: and this choice, which destiny creates in man, he had made in awareness and courage. There lay all his joy in living and dying" (199–200). He goes on to say that the fear of death is the greatest obstacle to living; only in accepting death can one know the fullness of life.

Camus's other murderers explore different facets of this insight. Caligula concludes from the death of his beloved Drusilla that life is absurd. Being supposedly divine, he chooses to behave like one of the gods, dealing death and pain as his whim dictates. He is the precise opposite of Meursault in one sense, for he has chosen in full consciousness to embody the absurd. Meursault, by contrast, seems at most to intuit the philosophical implications of the absurd. Yet they act in similar fashion. Caligula, like Meursault, calls for his own execution at the end. The "renegade" also tries to ally himself with divine forces, and kills in their name. The life of pain and deprivation he has known could justify his belief that violence was divine law. Camus endows the "renegade" at his death with unmistakable Christ-like qualities, although most critics have judged him even less Christ-like than Meursault.

In one form or another Camus's murderers seem to believe that since the natural law of the universe is that all living things must die, they are following that law by killing. They discover that they are wrong, however. As humans, they have a power to seek meaning in opposition to the absurd that is the law of nature. If they fail to seek that meaning, they miss the essential quality of human life. In fact, at the point of death, they recognize what they have missed previously, and even with only minutes to live they find a form of joy and reconciliation.

THE QUEST FOR MEANING

Meursault, in reliving the days between his mother's death and his murder of the Arab, reconstructs an innocence for himself. Readers have divided over whether the Meursault of part 1 is a man who simply lacks curiosity and introspection, or whether he has chosen to withdraw within a shell of deliberate indifference and passivity. The latter version seems to depict a far more culpable character by normal standards: one who presumably knew what he was doing but refused to care. The former version allows the construction of a defense on grounds of ignorance. From the perspective of the narrating Meursault, however, neither of these postures is acceptable. Camus, through Meursault, appears in fact to have created a deliberate ambiguity, so as to allow either interpretation. For Meursault's ultimate revelation can accommodate either.

It makes no difference whatsoever to the Meursault of the last page whether the Meursault of part 1 is guilty or not guilty by some external definition. A system of justice has pronounced him guilty; any reader can find much to say in his defense. But his joy and his innocence arise from his affirmation of his own life, not from any such criteria as judicial guilt. These are precisely the sorts of notions that he finds meaningless. In his final rage against the chaplain, he lays claim to the life he has led, the only value he has: "I had lived my life one way and I could just as well have lived it another. I had done this and I hadn't done that. I hadn't done this thing but I had done another. And so? It was as if I had waited all this time for this moment and for the first light of this dawn to be vindicated" (121; GS 151–152). That dawn is, of course, the summons to the guillotine; it is his own death that confers innocence upon his life. And since all must die, all may claim that state of innocence. For Meursault, the realization of this truth puts him in a state of grace.

As an ethical position, this eleventh-hour illumination entails many difficulties. It is no doubt in part for that reason that Camus returned to the theme so often. Meursault's answer serves only for the individual and offers no guidance for action. It retains its power for readers in the 1980s, because it still remains a necessary first step in a quest for truth and for happiness in an absurd world.

For citizens of the Western nations, the universe may well seem a more hospitable place in the late 1980s than it did to Camus and his contemporaries. That may explain in part why it seems less urgent now to explain and justify the moral philosophy implied in *The Stranger*. We can accept its flaws, because our attention falls elsewhere, on the ways in which Meursault struggles to make sense, and on the ways in which Camus represents this struggle. The answer Camus intended matters less than how he arrived at it, or more accurately, how he drew the reader into the quest.

We have seen instances where the act of interpretation is dramatized in *The Stranger*. It happens at all levels. The book begins with Meursault trying to decipher a telegram. He labors throughout part 1 to make enough sense of his surroundings to survive, or to justify his inability to make sense. In part 2 he is forced willy-nilly to participate in interpretation on a grand scale. His whole life, the social order, and entire systems of belief are called into question at his trial and in the attendant incidents. This movement explains the differences between the two halves, not only in Meursault's perspective but in Camus's. Part 1 tries to represent the world as it is, which is to say extremely individualized and concrete. Part 2, by contrast, represents the process of interpretation. There, the reality depicted becomes more abstract and less credible, because Camus apparently wanted us to sense that, like Meursault, we all live under an absurd sentence of death, that we are all prisoners of our material existence.

Whether or not we follow Meursault and Camus to the end of their line of thought, *The Stranger* presents a challenging portrayal of the quest. Of course, part 1 cannot represent the world as it is; it can only represent a world already interpreted by Meursault, and by Camus. The greatness of Camus's conception lies partly in the fact that Meursault seems to anticipate our anxieties. He has no confidence in his own representation of reality. Every affirmation seems to contain its own denial, every conclusion its own criticism. Meursault agonizes over language and its failures. He surrenders repeatedly to the temptation of silence, but makes one heroic breakthrough in the final chapter, which enables him to articulate his story from the funeral to the execution. *The Stranger* survives as a living masterpiece in the 1980s because it still speaks to our doubts and concerns. Meursault need not be a hero to us; Camus's moral philosophy need not win our adherence. But *The Stranger* is a novel in which the interplay of elusive reality and its always imperfect interpretation still engage us and command our attention.

BIBLIOGRAPHY

Primary Works

Collected Editions in French

Théâtre, récits, nouvelles. Edited by Roger Quilliot. Bibliothèque de la Pléiade. Paris: Gallimard, 1962. An authoritative edition, with introductions, notes, variants, and complementary texts. This volume has been reprinted several times since the first edition in 1962, and some later printings contain revisions and additions, which alter the page numbering.

Essais. Edited by Roger Quilliot. Bibliothèque de la Pléiade. Paris: Gallimard, 1965.

Editions of *L'Étranger* and Uncollected Works in French

L'Étranger. Paris: Gallimard, 1942. A slightly revised version was published in 1953 and is now the standard French text; the English translation by Stuart Gilbert was based on the first edition, the one by Matthew Ward on the standard text.

L'Étranger. Edited by Germaine Brée and Carlos Lynes, Jr. New York: Appleton-Century-Crofts, 1955. An American textbook edition, expurgated and not reliable as a text, but with an interesting introduction by the editors and an important foreword written by Camus for this edition, reprinted in the Pléiade edition but not in other French editions.

La Mort heureuse. Edited by Jean Sarocchi. *Cahiers Albert Camus,* vol. 1. Paris: Gallimard, 1971. Posthumous first publication of Camus's first novel; despite a hero named Mersault and some passages copied verbatim in *L'Étranger,* this is a different novel, and not a first draft.

English Translations

Caligula and Three Other Plays. Translated by Stuart Gilbert. Paperback ed. New York: Vintage Books, 1962. Includes *The Misunderstanding, State of Siege,* and *The Just Assassins.*

Exile and the Kingdom. Translated by Justin O'Brien. Paperback ed. New York: Vintage Books, 1957.

The Fall. Translated by Justin O'Brien. Paperback ed. New York: Vintage Books, 1957.

A Happy Death. Translated by Richard Howard. New York: Alfred A. Knopf, 1972.

Lyrical and Critical Essays. Edited with notes by Philip Thody. Translated by Ellen Conroy Kennedy. New York: Alfred A. Knopf, 1968. Includes *L'Envers et l'endroit,* 1937; *Noces,* 1938; *L'Été,* 1954; and other essays from the Pléiade edition.

The Myth of Sisyphus and Other Essays. Translated by Justin O'Brien. New York: Vintage Books/Random House, 1955. Includes *Le Mythe de Sisyphe,* 1942; essays from *Noces,* 1938; and *L'Été,* 1954; and part of an interview.

The Plague. Translated by Stuart Gilbert. Paperback ed. New York: Vintage Books, 1972.

The Rebel: An Essay on Man in Revolt. Translation by Anthony Bower of *L'Homme révolté.* Foreword by Sir Herbert Read. Rev. ed. New York: Alfred A. Knopf, 1978. First published in 1954; new copyright 1956; eleventh printing 1978.

Resistance, Rebellion, and Death. Translated with an introduction by Justin O'Brien. New York: Alfred A. Knopf, 1961. Includes essays from *Lettres à un ami allemand,* 1948; *Actuelles,* 1950; *Actuelles II,* 1953; *Actuelles III,* 1958; *Réflexions sur la peine capitale,* 1957; *Discours de Suède,* 1958; plus interviews.

The Stranger. Translated by Stuart Gilbert. New York: Alfred A. Knopf, 1946. Paperback ed. New York: Vintage Books/Random House, 1954.

The Stranger. Translated with a note by Matthew Ward. New York: Alfred A. Knopf, 1988.

Bibliography

Secondary Works

Bibliographies

Alden, Douglas W.; Hoy, Peter C.; and Zunz, Christine M., editors. *French XX Bibliography*. New York: French Institute/Alliance Française, 1949––. An annual list of criticism and scholarship on twentieth-century French literature. The first volumes were called *French VII Bibliography*. The editors, sponsors, and publishers have varied. The latest issue, vol. 37 for 1985, announces that vol. 38 will be published by the Susquehanna University Press. This list is the most convenient and complete supplement to the 1980 Cabeen critical bibliography for works that have appeared since it went to press.

Beebe, Maurice. "Criticism of Albert Camus: A Selected Checklist of Studies in English." *Modern Fiction Studies* 10 (1964):303–14. Special Issue on Albert Camus. Outdated, but sometimes useful since it is limited to works in English. Updated by Margaret Church et al. in "Five Modern French Novelists: A Bibliography." *Modern Fiction Studies* 16 (1970):85–100.

Fitch, Brian T., and Hoy, Peter C. *Calepins de bibliographie I: Albert Camus 1*. 3d ed. Paris: Lettres Modernes Minard, 1972. Lists only works in French, tabulated year by year.

Gay-Crosier, Raymond, editor. "Camus." In *The Twentieth Century,* edited by Douglas W. Alden and Richard A. Brooks, pt. 3, chap. 34, pp. 1573-1679, nos. 14426–15572. In *A Critical Bibliography of French Literature*, vol. 6, edited by David Clark Cabeen. Syracuse: Syracuse University Press, 1980. The best place to begin any research on Camus; classified and annotated list of works on Camus by one of the best informed scholars in the field.

MLA International Bibliography. New York: Modern Language Association, 1922––. An annual list of scholarship and criticism about literature. Extensive coverage of periodicals, but does not include reviews and coverage of books is less systematic. Its chief advantages are that recent years are indexed in several ways, including subject and language of the work listed, and that the bibliography is also available as a database and can be searched on-line through DIALOG INFORMATION SERVICES and its subsidiary KNOWLEDGE INDEX.

Revue des Lettres Modernes: Albert Camus. Paris: Lettres Modernes Minard. *Revue des Lettres Modernes* is an irregular periodical, of which each issue is devoted to one author. *Albert Camus 12: La Révolte en question* appeared in 1985. Each issue contains a bibliographical section, reviewing the most recent work on Camus. All articles and reviews are in French.

Roeming, Robert F. *Camus: A Bibliography*. 5th ed., microfiche. Milwaukee: Computing Services of the University of Wisconsin, 1976. A computer-generated list of works by and about Camus.

Books in English

Banks, G. V. *Camus: "L'Étranger"*. London: Edward Arnold, 1976. A brief introductory study, focusing on style and on Meursault's character.

Brée, Germaine. *Camus*. New Brunswick, N.J.: Rutgers University Press, 1959. General study of Camus's life and works; chapter on *The Stranger* treats Meursault as a heroic figure.

Brée, Germaine, ed. *Camus: A Collection of Critical Essays*. "Twentieth Century Views." Englewood Cliffs, N.J.: Prentice-Hall, 1962. A very useful collection of essays, including Sartre's "Explication of *The Stranger*."

Champigny, Robert J. *A Pagan Hero: An Interpretation of Meursault in Camus's "The Stranger"*. Translated by Rowe Portis. Philadelphia: University of Pennsylvania Press, 1969. Originally published as *Sur un héros païen*. Paris: Gallimard, 1960. A study of Meursault's character; takes the unusual stance of treating the novel's world as real, discussing it from within.

Cruickshank, John. *Albert Camus and the Literature of Revolt*. New York: Oxford University Press, 1960. Study of Camus's works, with emphasis on the ideas.

Fitch, Brian T. *The Narcissistic Text: A Reading of Camus' Fiction*. Toronto: University of Toronto Press, 1982. A collection of articles; chapter 4, "The Hermeneutic Paradigm: *L'Étranger*," studies the novel as a model of interpretive activity.

Grenier, Roger, ed. *Album Camus*. Paris: Gallimard, 1982. Iconography; almost five hundred illustrations relating to Camus's life and works. Text in French.

Jones, Rosemarie. *"L'Étranger" and "La Chute"*. London: Grant & Cutler, 1980. An introductory essay on the two novels.

King, Adele. *Camus*. Edinburgh and London: Oliver & Boyd, 1964. General introduction to Camus, with a chapter on *The Stranger*.

Lazere, Donald. *The Unique Creation of Albert Camus*. New Haven and London: Yale University Press, 1973. A study of Camus's works, with political and psychoanalytical perspectives on *The Stranger*.

Lottman, Herbert R. *Albert Camus: A Biography*. Garden City, N.Y.: Doubleday, 1979. An impressively documented biography, much the most complete.

McCarthy, Patrick. *Camus: A Critical Study of His Life and Work*. London: Hamish Hamilton, 1982. Interesting and somewhat polemical biography, with a special focus on Algeria and Camus's political positions.

O'Brien, Conor Cruise. *Camus*. London: Fontana/Collins, 1970. An essay with a political perspective, critical of Camus.

Rhein, Phillip H. *Albert Camus*. Twayne World Authors Series. New York: Twayne, 1969. Very useful brief survey of Camus's life, works, and ideas.

Rizzuto, Anthony. *Camus' Imperial Vision*. Carbondale and Edwardsville: Southern Illinois University Press, 1981. An account of the evolution of

Camus's thought, taking *The Stranger* as a bleak vision of isolation, leading to a sense of human community in the later works.
Thody, Philip. *Albert Camus, 1913–1960*. New York: Macmillan, 1962. General study of Camus, with a chapter on *The Stranger*; tends to support
Camus's remarks on Meursault as a heroic figure.

Books in French

Barrier, M.-G. *L'Art du récit dans "l'Étranger" d'Albert Camus*. Paris: Nizet,
1962. An study emphasizing the style and narrative technique.
Bonnier, Henry. *Albert Camus ou la force d'être*. Lyon-Paris: Vitte, 1959. Interesting as one of the few studies to argue that *The Stranger* should be
read as a day-by-day journal, not a retrospective.
Castex, Pierre-Georges. *Albert Camus et "L'Étranger"*. Paris: José Corti,
1965. Study of sources and composition of the novel, and analysis of
Meursault.
Eisenzweig, Uri. *Les Jeux de l'écriture dans "L'Étranger" de Camus*. Archives
des Lettres Modernes, no. 211; Archives Albert Camus, no. 6. Paris:
Lettres Modernes Minard, 1983. A study of *The Stranger* by a disciple of
Gérard Genette and of the Geneva School; sees Meursault as a voice opposed to the written.
Fitch, Brian T. *"L'Étranger" d'Albert Camus: un texte, ses lecteurs, leurs lec-
tures*. Paris: Librairie Larousse, 1972. An exceptionally useful book,
which summarizes the major interpretations of *The Stranger* and then
proposes its own, concentrating on the reader's role. Contains an extensive annotated bibliography.
———. *Narrateur et narration dans "L'Étranger" d'Albert Camus*. Archives
des Lettres Modernes 34. 2d ed. rev. and enl. Paris: Lettres Modernes
Minard, 1968. Groundbreaking analysis of narrative technique and reading the novel; Fitch has incorporated its insights into later works.
Gay-Crosier, Raymond, editor. *Albert Camus 1980*. Gainesville: University
Presses of Florida, 1980. Collection of papers from a conference on Camus; several deal with *The Stranger*.
Gay-Crosier, Raymond, and Lévi-Valensi, Jacqueline, eds. *Albert Camus:
œuvre fermée, œuvre ouverte?* Actes du Colloque du Centre Culturel International de Cerisy-la-Salle, 18–28 June 1982. Cahiers Albert Camus,
no. 5. Paris: Gallimard, 1985. A collection of papers from a colloquium
devoted to Camus; includes several psychoanalytical interpretations of
The Stranger and others using new critical approaches.

Articles and Chapters in Books in English

Amash, Paul J. "The Choice of an Arab in *L'Étranger.*" *Romance Notes* 10 (1967):2–5. Argues that Camus made the murder victim an Arab so that the death penalty would seem motivated by other reasons.

Atkins, Anselm. "Fate and Freedom: Camus' *The Stranger.*" *Renascence* 21 (1969):64–75, 110. Discusses the interplay between fate and freedom.

Barthes, Roland. "Writing and Silence." In *Writing Degree Zero and Elements of Semiology,* translated by Annette Lavers and Colin Smith, 62–65. London: Jonathan Cape, 1984. Major essay by one of the leading critics and theorists of the twentieth century.

Bersani, Leo. "The Stranger's Secrets." *Novel* 3 (1970):212–14. Reprint. In *Balzac to Beckett: Center and Circumference in French Fiction,* 247–72. New York: Oxford University Press, 1970. Compares *The Stranger* to the French *nouveau roman*; finds Camus more classical.

Falk, Eugene. "*L'Étranger.*" In *Types of Thematic Structure: The Nature and Function of Motifs in Gide, Camus and Sartre,* 52–116. Chicago: University of Chicago Press, 1967. Detailed analysis of themes.

Feuerlicht, Ignace. "Camus's *L'Étranger* Reconsidered." *PMLA* 78 (1963):606–21. Reviews critical problems and debates.

Fitch, Brian T. "Aesthetic Distance and Inner Space in the Novels of Camus." *Modern Fiction Studies* 10 (1964):279–92. On narrative problems and their effects on interpretation.

Fletcher, Dennis. "Camus between Yes and No: A Fresh Look at the Murder in *L'Étranger.*" *Neophilologus* 61 (1977):523–33. Relates the murder to Camus's autobiographical essays, especially the creative son and the silent unintellectual mother; sees the murder as symbolic moment of choice between action and regression.

Fletcher, John. "Interpreting *L'Étranger.*" *French Review* 43 (1970):158–67. Emphasizes the oedipal myth, erotic elements in the account of the murder, and Meursault as a tragic hero.

————. "Meursault's Rhetoric." *Critical Quarterly* 13 (1971):125–36. Studies use of tenses; concludes that Meursault narrates from a moment after his appeal has been rejected and tries to appeal to readers.

Frohock, Wilbur M. "Albert Camus in *L'Étranger.*" In *Style and Temper. Studies in French Fiction, 1925–1960,* 103–115. Cambridge: Harvard University Press, 1967. Analysis of the metaphors in the murder scene and of the outburst against the chaplain.

Gale, John E. "Does America Know *The Stranger*? A Reappraisal of a Translation." *Modern Fiction Studies* 20 (1974):139–47. Critical analysis of the Stuart translation.

Girard, René. "Camus's Stranger Retried." *PMLA* 79 (1964):519–33. Reprint. In *"To Double Business Bound",* 9–35. Baltimore: Johns Hopkins University Press, 1978. Deflates Meursault's status as a hero and treats *The Fall* as a superior rewriting of *The Stranger.*

Kamber, Gerald. "The Allegory of Names in *L'Étranger.*" *Modern Language Quarterly* 22 (1961):292–301. Studies the symbolism of characters' names; includes a letter from Camus denying any conscious symbolism.

Kazin, Alfred. "Rebel and Stranger." Review of *Camus* by Patrick McCarthy. *New Republic*, 29 November 1982, 33–35.

Krieger, Murray. "Albert Camus: Beyond Nonentity and the Rejection of the Tragic." In *The Tragic Vision*, 144–53. New York: Holt, Rinehart, & Winston, 1960. Discusses Meursault as an anti-tragic hero, a man without guilt, Camus's vision of an atheistic humanism.

Lehan, Richard. "Camus' American Affinities." *Symposium* 13 (1959):255–70. Discusses the influence of American novelists on Camus.

———. "Levels of Reality in the Novels of Albert Camus." *Modern Fiction Studies* 10 (1964):232–44. Compares *The Stranger* to American novels, especially works of Theodore Dreiser and James M. Cain.

Leites, Nathan. "The Stranger." In *Art and Psychoanalysis,* edited by William Phillips, 247–67. New York: Criterion, 1963. A balanced and nontechnical psychoanalytical reading of the novel, which tries less to find a key to the text in Camus's subconscious than to show Meursault's psychological plausibility.

Madden, David. "Camus' *The Stranger*: An Achievement in Simultaneity." *Renascence* 20 (1967–68):86–97. Emphasizes the religious aspects of the novel, including Meursault as a Christ figure.

Manly, William M. "Journey to Consciousness: The Symbolic Pattern of Camus's *L'Étranger.*" *PMLA* 79 (1964):321–28. Expands on Sartre's linking of *The Stranger* and *The Myth of Sisyphus*; an important study of the ideas in the novel.

Matthews, J. H. "From *The Stranger* to *The Fall*: Confession and Complicity." *Modern Fiction Studies* 10 (1964):265–78. Compares the two novels.

Molnar, Thomas. "Albert Camus: Guide of a Generation." *Catholic World* 186, no. 1, 114, (January 1958):272–77.

Nuttall, A. D. "Did Meursault Mean to Kill the Arab? The Intentional Fallacy Fallacy." *Critical Quarterly* 10 (1968):95–106. A discussion of Meursault's act and his responsibility for it, in the framework of the debate in critical theory over the author's intention and its relevance to aesthetic analysis.

O'Brien, Justin, and Roudiez, Leon S. "Camus." *Saturday Review,* 13 February 1960, 19–21 ff.

Robbe-Grillet, Alain. "Nature, Humanism, Tragedy." In *For a New Novel: Essays on Fiction,* translated by Richard Howard, 49–75. New York: Grove Press, 1965. Brief but incisive comments on *The Stranger* by a leading practitioner of the *nouveau roman* denying that the novel depicts real separation between humans and things.

Rose, Marilyn Gaddis. "Meursault as Pharmakos: A Reading of *L'Étranger.*"

Modern Fiction Studies 10 (1964):258–64. Discusses Meursault in the context of the myth of the scapegoat.

Ross, Stephen David. "*The Stranger* by Albert Camus." In *Literature and Philosophy: An Analysis of the Philosophical Novel,* 175–196. New York: Appleton-Century-Crofts, 1969. Argues that *The Stranger* poses the philosophical problem of the absurd, but does not propose a solution.

Roudiez, Leon S. "The Literary Climate of *L'Étranger*: Sample of a Twentieth-Century Atmosphere." *Symposium* 12 (1958):19–35. Special issue on Albert Camus. Discusses affinities between Camus's novel and works of five contemporary French writers: Alain, Bernanos, Aragon, Saint-Exupéry, and Malraux.

Sandstrom, Glenn. "The Outsiders of Stendhal and Camus." *Modern Fiction Studies* 10 (1964):245–57. Compares Meursault to the hero of Stendhal's *The Red and the Black,* Julien Sorel.

Sarraute, Nathalie. "From Dostoievski to Kafka." In *The Age of Suspicion: Essays on the Novel,* translated by Maria Jolas, 17–24. New York: Braziller, 1963. Discussion of *The Stranger* by another leading practitioner of the *nouveau roman,* which criticizes the ending on grounds of narrative theory.

Sartre, Jean-Paul. "Camus' *The Outsider*." In *Literary and Philosophical Essays of Jean-Paul Sartre,* translated by Annette Michelson, 24–41. New York: Criterion, 1955. Retitled "An Explication of *The Stranger*." In *Camus: A Collection of Critical Essays,* edited by Germaine Brée, 108–121. Essential essay, stressing the novel's ideas and its connections to *The Myth of Sisyphus.*

Sebba, Helen. "Stuart Gilbert's Meursault: A Strange 'Stranger.'" *Contemporary Literature* 13 (1972):334–40. A critical discussion of the English translation.

Solatoroff, Theodore. "Camus's Portable Pedestal." *New Republic,* 21 December 1968, 27–30.

Stamm, Julian L. "Camus's *Stranger*: His Act of Violence." *American Imago* 26 (1969):281–90. Psychoanalytical study, arguing that Meursault's character has sadistic and homosexual elements.

Thody, Philip. "Camus's *L'Étranger* Revisited." *Critical Quarterly* 21 (1979):61–69. A sensible discussion of Meursault's racism, the degree to which it can also be imputed to Camus, and its effect on our interpretation of the novel.

Ullman, Stephen. "The Two Styles of Camus: *L'Étranger*." In *The Image in the Modern French Novel,* 244–54. Cambridge: Cambridge University Press, 1960. Study of the images in *The Stranger.*

Viggiani, Carl A. "Camus's *L'Étranger*." *PMLA* 71 (1956):865–87. One of the first and best studies of the structures, themes, and symbols.

Wagner, C. Roland. "The Silence of *The Stranger*." *Modern Fiction Studies* 10

(1964):27–40. Argues that Meursault is not detached and not a martyr to sincerity; suggests that Meursault's silence reflects Camus's own silence regarding unresolved problems in his thought.

Articles and Chapters in Books in French

Barthes, Roland. "*L'Étranger,* roman solaire." *Club* 12 (April 1954):7. Reprinted in *Les Critiques de notre temps et Camus,* edited by Jacqueline Lévi-Valensi, 60–64. Paris: Garnier, 1970. Brief essay by a major critic, evoking the mythic role of the sun.

Coquet, J.-C. "Problèmes de l'analyse structurale du récit *L'Étranger* d'Albert Camus." *Langue Française* 3 (1969):61–72. Attempt, via linguistic and structuralist theories of Saussure, Benveniste, and Greimas, to discover the deep structure of the novel.

Cornille, Jean-Louis. "Blanc, semblant et vraisemblance: Sur l'incipit de *L'Étranger.*" *Littérature* 23 (1976):49–55. Deconstructs the first lines of the novel, to show that the first statement, by its very formulation, is the revelation of a contradictory response.

Goldschlager, Alain, and Lemaire, Jacques. "Technique parataxique et psychologie des personnages dans *L'Étranger.*" *Neophilologus* 61 (1977):185–93. Analysis of parataxis, or absence of linking words.

Pichon-Rivière, Arminda A. de, and Baranger, Willy. "Répression du deuil et intensification des mécanismes et des angoisses schizo-paranoïdes (notes sur *L'Étranger* d'Albert Camus)." *Revue Française de Psychanalyse* 23 (1959):409–20. Psychoanalytical study of the novel, arguing that Meursault's schizo-paranoid tendencies prevent his successfully mourning his mother's death.

Quinn, Renée. "Le Thème racial dans *L'Étranger.*" *Revue d'Histoire Littéraire de la France* 69 (1969):1009–13. A political reading of *The Stranger,* stressing the racist and colonialist elements.

Soelberg, Nils. "Le Paradoxe du 'je'-narrateur: Approche narratologique de *L'Étranger* de Camus." *Revue Romane* 20 (1985):68–97. Narratological analysis, arguing that the ambiguity of the narrative moment is intended to call attention to the paradox that the importance of Meursault's life is its unimportance, hence the narration must deny the importance it automatically confers on the narrated.

Vigée, Claude. "L'Errance entre 'L'Exil et le Royaume.'" *Table Ronde* 146 (February 1960):120–26. On the murder as a ritual act.

INDEX

Index

Index

Index

ABOUT THE AUTHOR

English Showalter, Jr., received his doctorate in French from Yale University in 1964. He has taught at Haverford College, the University of California at Davis, Princeton University, and Rutgers University, Camden, where he is currently professor of French and chair of the French department. From 1983 to 1985 he was Executive Director of the Modern Language Association. He is the author of *Exiles and Strangers: A Reading of Camus's "Exile and the Kingdom"*, published by the Ohio State University Press in 1984, as well as articles on Camus. He has also written extensively about other areas of French literature, especially eighteenth-century. His books include *The Evolution of the French Novel, 1641–1782* (Princeton, N.J.: Princeton University Press, 1972) and two studies, on Voltaire and on Rousseau, based on the letters of Françoise de Graffigny. He is part of a team working on a multivolume edition of the Graffigny letters and literary advisor for the project. The first volume was published in 1985 by the Voltaire Foundation; volumes are scheduled to appear annually. The edition will include about twelve volumes.